PARLIAMENTARY HISTORY: TEXTS & STUDIES

11

Sir Thomas Duppa's Commonplace Book

T0385864

Sir Thomas Duppa c.1685 in his robes as gentleman usher of the order of the garter and holding his eponymous black rod painted by Willem Wissing (*d*. 1687) and workshop. Parliamentary Art Collection, Works of Art 7170 © Palace of Westminster.

Sir Thomas Duppa's Commonplace Book

Edited by

Alasdair Hawkyard and J.C. Sainty

Wiley Blackwell

for

The Parliamentary History Yearbook Trust

This edition first published 2015

© 2015 Parliamentary History Yearbook Trust

Registered Office

John Wiley & Sons Ltd, The Atrium, Southern Gate, Chichester, West Sussex, PO19 8SQ, UK

Editorial Offices

350 Main Street, Malden, MA 02148-5020, USA

9600 Garsington Road, Oxford, OX4 2DQ, UK

The Atrium, Southern Gate, Chichester, West Sussex, PO19 8SQ, UK

For details of our global editorial offices, for customer services, and for information about how to apply for permission to reuse the copyright material in this book please see our website at www.wiley.com/wiley-blackwell.

Library of Congress Cataloging-in-Publication Data

Duppa, Thomas, 1619–1694, author.

 Sir Thomas Duppa's commonplace book / edited by Alasdair Hawkyard and J.C. Sainty.

  pages cm

 Book originally compiled by Sir Thomas Duppa for his own use.

 Includes bibliographical references and index.

 ISBN 978-1-119-08599-7 (alk. paper)

 1. Great Britain. Parliament. House of Lords–History–17th century. 2. Black Rod. I. Hawkyard, Alasdair, editor. II. Sainty, John Christopher, editor. III. Parliamentary History Yearbook Trust, issuing body. IV. Title.

 JN621.D86 2015

 328.41′07109031

                                                                                  2015031989

A catalogue record for this book is available from the British Library.

Set in size 10/12 Pt Bembo

Printed in Singapore

1 2015

CONTENTS

ACKNOWLEDGMENTS

While doing some work in the library at the Royal Society, Charles Littleton of the History of Parliament noticed a reference to a document, MS 70, then believed to be a compilation by the clerk of the parliaments. Closer inspection revealed it to be a commonplace book kept by black rod. Unable to pursue its study himself, Littleton drew the notice of his friend Clyve Jones to the commonplace book. In his turn Jones brought it to the attention of Sir John Sainty and Alasdair Hawkyard and persuaded them to undertake its transcription, editing and publication for *Parliamentary History*'s Texts & Studies series. The Royal Society readily and kindly agreed to this project.

At the Royal Society the archivist, Joanna Corden, and the library staff, Rupert Baker, Fiona Keates and Keith Moore were exemplary in their kindness and helpfulness. Special mention should be made of Fiona Keates who explained how little was known about Francis Aston, an early secretary to the Royal Society, and one time owner of the commonplace book, but who then went on to suggest sources which revealed precisely the circumstances of the arrival of the commonplace book there.

Melanie Unwin of the Parliamentary Art Collection arranged a viewing of the Willem Wissing portrait of Sir Thomas Duppa which had been acquired by the collection in 2011.

Andrew Barclay with his knowledge of the mid-Stuart court and household helped elucidate the identity of Thomas Boreman.

METHOD

The layout follows the manuscript with the original pagination given on the left-hand side. Several sections are left un-paginated in the manuscript, and for these a modern descriptive phrase reflecting their position and occurrence has been adopted.

For the most part abbreviations and contractions have been extended. The designation of the clerkship of the parliaments held successively by John Browne and Matthew Johnson posed a problem as the two men clearly employed slightly different variants during their tenure of the post and Johnson was inconsistent in his practice.

Additions are given in square brackets.

Where the entry in the commonplace book is identical with that in the *Lords Journal* the entry is briefly calendared with the reference in the printed *Lords Journal* provided. Such calendared entries are given in italics.

ABBREVIATIONS

BM	British Museum
CJ	*Commons Journal*
CTB	*Calendar of Treasury Books*
d	dorse (of membranes)
HKW	*The History of the King's Works*, ed. H.M. Colvin *et al.* (6 vols, 1963–82)
HPC, 1660–1690	*History of Parliament, The House of Commons 1660–1690*, ed. B.D. Henning (3 vols, 1983)
HPC, 1690–1715	*History of Parliament, The House of Commons 1690–1715*, ed. E. Cruickshanks, S. Handley and D.W. Hayton (5 vols, Cambridge, 2002)
HPC, 1715–1754	*History of Parliament, The House of Commons 1715–1754*, ed. R. Sedgwick (2 vols, 1970)
LJ	*Lords Journal*
ODNB	*Oxford Dictionary of National Biography*
ORH	*Officials of the Royal Household 1660–1837*, ed. J.C. Sainty and R.O. Bucholz (2 vols, 1997, 1998)
rots	rotulets
RWA	*The Marriage, Baptismal and Burial Registers of the Collegiate Church or Abbey of St Peter, Westminster Abbey*, ed. J.L. Chester (Harleian Society, 1876)
TNA	The National Archives, Kew

Introduction

Royal Society MS 70 is a bound paper volume with a pair of board covers covered with vellum. Originally it was kept secure with two sets of green ties. The measurements of the pages are 13¼ × 9 inches (33.2 × 21.2 cm). On the right-hand side there is a red margin set in 1¹⁴⁄₁₅ inches (4.8 cm).

The first 133 pages are paginated continuously followed by a single unnumbered page with three entries. Towards the end of the volume there are further entries on seven unnumbered pages, with the sequence of material starting at the end, the book having been turned upside down. There are also two loose items, both unnumbered sheets, one of these being inscribed '57', which may refer to its original position in another, lost volume.

Close scrutiny of the manuscript reveals that it is a copy of a text no longer extant. Up to and including page 133 it is the work of a single person with no sign of any interruption or breaks. Some marginalia and headings were inserted by another person or more on completion of the main task. Several additions were later made by Francis Aston.

The sentence 'NB Here was Mr Churchill the Stationers Two Bills'[1] reveals that the copy is not an exact one. However, the extent of the copyist's departures from the original document is difficult to gauge, but evidently in the original some of the entries lacked headings which someone then made good.[2] He did, however, preserve a now otherwise meaningless '4' on page 46. Had contemporary practice been followed, changes in subject would have occasioned a fresh page. For example, the heading for the list of wood and candles in late spring and early summer 1688 appears at the bottom of page 83 but the list itself is on the following page. There are a handful of errors in copying, some of which were picked up by whoever checked the work.

The volume is entitled, on a small piece of paper glued to its spine, 'House of Lords Clerk's Book' (2013). Following J.O. Halliwell's *A Catalogue of the Miscellaneous Manuscripts Preserved in the Library of the Royal Society* (1840), it is described in the current catalogue as 'a Notebook of the clerk of the house of lords, 1660–69'. This description reflects very well on Halliwell's erudition, but is not quite correct.

The contents certainly relate largely to the house of lords. However, they are concerned principally with the activities of the gentleman usher of the black rod, with the clerk making only incidental appearances. The bulk of the entries relate to the years 1676–94, which coincide with the period when (Sir) Thomas Duppa was active in the office of black rod, first as deputy 1675–83 and then as principal 1683–94. The presence of certain items of earlier date is probably to be explained by their value as precedents.[3] From 1689 Duppa is the recipient of a sequence of communications from the clerk of

---

[1] Royal Society, London, MS 70, p. 108.

[2] An omission concerned the allowance paid to Richard Sparrow for his attendance in the house of lords in 1685 (p. 58).

[3] Royal Society, MS 70, pp. 3–4, 35–6, 62–3.

the parliaments conveying the orders of the house of lords principally for the attachment or release of delinquents. The last of these is dated 12 February 1694, two months before Duppa's death.[4]

The bulk of the material relates directly to Duppa. The first item relates to the fees paid by the earl of Ossory on his installation as a knight of the garter[5] which occurred four years before Duppa's appointment as deputy. The next item is the attachment of the duke of Buckingham in 1677.[6] The third item relates to fees paid to Carteret in 1678.[7] Thereafter the material follows a basic chronological progression until 1681.[8] There are then two throwbacks to 1666 ('The Manner of the Triall of a Peer') and 1679 (various instructions to Duppa).[9] These two throwbacks create the presumption that Duppa intended from the start to keep a handbook for his own use but initially was uncertain how to do so. From page 24 until page 125 the material is chronological with very occasional aberrations, usually to be explained by material seen by hindsight to be pertinent. The main areas covered can be listed: items relating to the order of the garter, fees and perquisites, salary ('pension'), the trials of peers, appointments, rituals and other ceremonial, coronations, maintenance of order in the Parliament House, fixtures and fittings there, fuel and stationery supplied, extraordinary disbursements, and a long-running dispute with the serjeant at arms over the responsibility for the handling of delinquents with its eventual resolution. Duppa also entered the orders received by him to convey peers and others to prison, to take custody of prisoners, to bring delinquents and others to the house of lords, to take custody of them and to discharge them when so authorised. These orders were made by the House and entered in the journal by the clerk of the parliaments. Duppa knew the wisdom of keeping a record of his own. Whether he was following a tradition established by his predecessors or the practice was an initiative of his own is not known.

The volume seems to have been laid aside during the tenure of Duppa's immediate successor Sir Fleetwood Sheppard since no material is recorded during his term of office 1694–8, but the presence of three orders of December 1699 during that of the next black rod, Sir David Mitchell, indicates a return to use. Mitchell had a deputy in the person of Francis Aston who stated in July 1700 that he had held this position 'for at least 3 years'.[10] How long Aston remained deputy is unclear. The last dated item of business recorded is of January 1704.[11]

For four years between 1681 and 1685 Aston had acted as one of the secretaries to the Royal Society. While he held this office, the Society authorised the making of copies of all its principal papers and the checking of these copies.[12] It looks as though Aston, inspired by the success of the practice at the Society, convinced Sir David

[4] Royal Society, MS 70, pp. 124–5.

[5] Royal Society, MS 70, pp. 1, 2.

[6] Royal Society, MS 70, pp. 3, 4.

[7] Royal Society, MS 70, p. 4.

[8] Royal Society, MS 70, pp. 6–11.

[9] Royal Society, MS 70, pp. 12–24.

[10] Royal Society, MS 70, p. Ai. See also *LJ*, xvi, 594–5; xvii, 158.

[11] Royal Society, MS 70, p. Avi.

[12] H.G. Lyons, 'Biographical Notes', *Notes and Records of the Royal Society*, iii (1940), 88–92; *ORH*, i, 68; Royal Society, minute book, ii, 52–3.

Mitchell of the need to adopt it in his own record keeping. Aston may not himself have been the person who checked the copy so produced but the survival there of his description of being passed over in favour of Oldes shows that he saw it sometime after completion. Aston was to examine the copy at least once more when he recorded on a separate sheet dated 1713 how Oldes came to be appointed black rod three years previously. The copy seems not to have remained among black rod's records as one might have expected but to have entered into Aston's working papers or personal possessions. While secretary of the Society he had kept in his possession copies of its journals and registers as well as many 'Originall papers'.[13] In his will dated 22 July 1715 he left the Society £50 in cash, the contents of his library (but not his personal writings) and the lands at Mablethorpe in Lincolnshire previously inherited from his elder brother.[14] Two weeks later Isaac Newton, the president, gave the executors a receipt for Aston's bequest.[15] The Society also paid Mr Aston's man four guineas for 'the trouble that he had been at in [its] service' over the will. Newton, together with Sir Hans Sloane and Edmund Halley, placed the books to 'the best advantage'.[16] A year later the Society rewarded its housekeeper, Alban Thomas, six guineas for cataloguing the books and making a copy for the executors, but he had to be upbraided another three years on for not having finished the job.[17] Although Thomas's catalogue no longer survives, there can be little doubt that the copy of the commonplace book entered the Society's ownership then, together with the rest of Aston's books. It had been numbered MS 70 by 1840 when it was listed in Halliwell's *A Catalogue*.

The interest of the volume resides principally in the light that it throws on the responsibilities and functions of black rod and other officials concerned with the administration of the palace of Westminster and parliament of which little evidence is to be found elsewhere at this date. Practically no records of black rod's office earlier than the 20th century survive in the custody of the Parliamentary Archives.[18] While black rod's public and ceremonial functions are sufficiently familiar his administrative duties are little known and the evidence supplied by this volume is therefore particularly welcome. At the same time information about his relations with other officials involved in the same field, notably the lord great chamberlain and the lord chamberlain, enable their significance to be better understood.

Notes on Select Officers

Black Rod

The gentleman usher of the black rod was in origin an officer of the order of the garter.[19] From the latter part of the 16th century the functions of usher of the parliament

---

[13] Royal Society, minutes of council, ii, 61.

[14] TNA, PROB 11/547, sig. 127.

[15] Royal Society, journal book, xii, 75.

[16] Royal Society, minutes of council, ii, 232.

[17] Royal Society, minutes of council, ii, 235, 249.

[18] M.F. Bond, *Guide to the Records of Parliament* (1971), 196.

[19] For this office, see Maurice Bond and David Beamish, *The Gentleman Usher of the Black Rod* (1976).

chamber or house of lords were exercised by one of the four gentleman ushers daily waiters in the royal household and it became customary for the crown to grant this usher the office of black rod as an additional perquisite. In 1631 it was formally decreed that this should be the invariable practice.[20] This step was taken because the office had passed into the hands of James Maxwell who, although he had been a gentleman usher when granted the reversion in 1617, had ceased to be such by the time he succeeded to the office of black rod in 1620. From the Restoration the decree of 1631 was strictly observed and all the holders of the office of black rod who feature in the volume were concurrently gentlemen ushers: Sir John Ayton (1661–71), Sir Edward Carteret (1671–83), Sir Thomas Duppa (1683–94) and Sir David Mitchell (1698–1710). As a general rule the office of black rod was considered to be a perquisite of the most senior gentleman usher. This was why Francis Aston felt aggrieved when William Oldes, who was junior to him in length of service, was placed above him in the household establishment list of 1702 and was eventually appointed black rod in 1710.[21]

While black rod continued to undertake the relatively undemanding duties of usher of the order of the garter, the bulk of his work related to the house of lords, which required his daily attendance and involved him in ceremony, notably the summoning of the house of commons and the introduction of newly created peers. The volume contains a detailed description of his duties in the chamber.[22] Black rod also acted as the disciplinary officer of the house, executing its orders for the attachment and release of delinquents, a function that he shared more or less unwillingly with the serjeant at arms.[23] In addition he acted as the channel through whom the house was supplied with its 'necessaries' – principally stationery, furniture and fuel.[24]

Black rod also acted as the agent of the lord great chamberlain. On one occasion Duppa described himself as 'Having the honour to be the immediate officer to your Lordship in the house of Peers'[25] and on another he received the lord great chamberlain's thanks 'for your kind and discrete Management of my Affairs in my Absence'.[26] Under the direction of the lord great chamberlain black rod took care of the chamber, prepared Westminster Hall for the trials of peers and performed numerous other services, notably ensuring 'that the Houses be searched according to the usual Custom' on the eve of the opening of a session.[27]

Apart from his parliamentary responsibilities black rod also had his duties as one of the four gentlemen ushers daily waiters in the royal household where he was subject to the lord chamberlain. In this capacity he attended the coronation[28] and administered the oath to servants of the bedchamber.[29]

---

[20] E. Ashmole, *The Institution, Laws and Ceremonies of the Most Noble Order of the Garter* (1672), 256.

[21] Royal Society, MS 70, loose item 1, d.

[22] Royal Society, MS 70, pp. 11–13, 19–23.

[23] Royal Society, MS 70, pp. 62–3, 87–91, 108–11.

[24] Royal Society, MS 70, pp. 9–10, 15–17, 42–4, 59–60, 65–8, 83–4, 126–30, Aii–iii, Avi.

[25] Royal Society, MS 70, p. 32.

[26] Royal Society, MS 70, pp. 57–8.

[27] Royal Society, MS 70, p. 11.

[28] Royal Society, MS 70, pp. 48, 50.

[29] Royal Society, MS 70, pp. 53–4.

In 1673 black rod's earlier forms of remuneration were commuted for a salary of £200 payable at the exchequer.[30] However, most of his income was apparently derived from fees arising on house of lords business[31] and from payments in kind, for example the scaffolds erected in Westminster Hall for the trial of peers.[32]

From time to time the crown appointed a deputy to black rod, during this period invariably one of the other gentlemen ushers daily waiters: Sir Edward Carteret to Sir John Ayton (1661), Thomas Duppa to Carteret (1675) and Francis Aston to Sir David Mitchell (1696 or 1697).[33]

Lord Great Chamberlain

The office of lord great chamberlain or chamberlain of England, one of the great offices of state, was long claimed by the family of de Vere, earls of Oxford, by hereditary right. Following the death of the 18th earl of Oxford in 1625 the succession was disputed by various claimants. In the event the office was awarded to Lord Willoughby de Eresby, Oxford's first cousin, who was created earl of Lindsey in 1626.[34] His grandson, Robert, the 3rd earl, who succeeded in 1666 and died in 1710, is the lord great chamberlain who features in this document.

By a process that remains to be clarified the lord great chamberlain came to exercise a wide jurisdiction in relation to the palace of Westminster and, more particularly, the house of lords. An account of his responsibilities in this area appears in the 20th edition of Edward Chamberlayne's *Angliae Notitia*, published in 1694, as follows:

> Moreover, to this Great Officer belongs the care of providing all things in the House of Lords in time of Parliament, and to that end he hath an Apartment near the *Lords House.*
>
> To him belongeth the Government of the whole Palace of *Westminster:* he issueth out his Warrants for the preparing, fitting and furnishing *Westminster-Hall* against *Coronations* and *Tryals of Peers* in *Parliament* time. The *Gentleman Usher of the Black Rod,* the *Yeoman-Usher* and *Door-keepers,* are under his Command.[35]

These are large claims but there is nothing in the document to contradict them. Indeed, it is one of its merits that it enables their validity to be assessed. The lord great chamberlain emerges as the pre-eminent officer where the palace and parliament are concerned. The evidence for this abounds but is perhaps most vividly illustrated in December 1688 when, following the proclamation for the meeting of parliament, it fell to the lord great chamberlain to authorise the lord chamberlain of the household to issue

---

[30] Royal Society, MS 70, pp. 38–9, 79–81; *CTB*, iv, 419.

[31] Royal Society, MS 70, pp. 3–5, 13–15, 81–2, Avi–vii.

[32] Royal Society, MS 70, pp. 27–32, 57.

[33] Royal Society, MS 70, pp. 35–6, 40–41, Ai.

[34] For this office, see *Complete Peerage*, ed. G.E.C. (2nd edn, 14 vols, 1910–98), x, Appendix F.

[35] E. Chamberlayne, *Angliae Notitia* (1694), pt 1, p. 156; see also *Report from the select committee of the house of lords on the office of gentleman usher of the black rod* (1906), p. iv, item 8.

his warrants to the relevant officials to make the necessary preparations.[36] Apart from the furnishing of the chamber he had responsibility for making the necessary arrangements for the trials of peers and the court of claims at coronations. As noted, in all these matters black rod acted as his agent.

Clerk of the Parliaments

The principal officer of the house of lords, known variously as clerk of the parliament or parliaments (*clericus parliamenti* or *parliamentorum*) was appointed by the crown by letters patent under the great seal. Among other things it was his function to transmit the orders made by the house to those whom they concerned and in particular to black rod. It is mainly in this capacity that he features in the document. John Browne, originally appointed clerk in 1638, was displaced on the abolition of the house in 1649. He returned to office at the Restoration in 1660, serving until his death in 1691. He was succeeded by Matthew Johnson who served until 1716.

Speaker of the House of Lords

The lord chancellor or lord keeper was speaker of the house of lords *ex officio* and presided whenever he was present. When the great seal was in commission the crown appointed a deputy or substitute, usually one of the judges of courts of common law, to take his place. In this way Sir Robert Atkyns, chief baron of the exchequer, served as Speaker 1689–93. In the absence of the lord chancellor or a substitute appointed by the crown the house chose its own Speaker. Thus the marquess of Halifax served during the convention of 1689.

It was customary for the lord chancellor to be appointed lord high steward to preside at the trials of peers as Lord Finch did at the trial of Lord Cornwallis in 1676.[37]

Serjeant at Arms

During the reign of Charles II a body of 16 serjeants at arms was attached to the court. In addition, there were serjeants at arms attached to particular officers of whom the lord chancellor was one.[38] Two holders of this office appear in the volume: Humphrey Leigh 1660–73 and Sir George Charnock 1673–84. Strictly speaking the lord chancellor's serjeant was assigned to him in his capacity as an officer of chancery, not as speaker of the house of lords. When the great seal was in commission the serjeant attended the commissioners and was therefore not available to serve the substitute speaker of the house of lords. This was the position between 1689 and 1693 when the office was held successively by the marquess of Halifax and Sir Robert Atkyns. In these circumstances Sir Roger Harsnett, one of the court serjeants, was detached to serve the Speaker. On

---

[36] Royal Society, MS 70, pp. 63–5.
[37] Royal Society, MS 70, pp. 24–5.
[38] *ORH*, i, 39.

his death in October 1692 his place was taken by Thomas Shirley, his successor as court serjeant, who served as long as Atkyns remained Speaker.

The serjeant's basic function was to accompany the Speaker with the mace but he also claimed the right to execute the orders of the House for the attachment of delinquents and to receive the fees for so doing. This brought him into conflict with black rod, who made a similar claim. In 1660 the Lords had declined to accede to the request that all such orders should be addressed to the serjeant and resolved to 'reserve the power to themselves to Imploy what Persons they shall think fit' for the purpose.[39] In practice the function was shared between black rod and the serjeant 'when the Lord Chancellor Hyde was the Great Minister of State'.[40] In December 1689 Harsnett's petition for the right to execute these orders was referred to the committee for privileges which also considered a counter-petition from Duppa rebutting his claim.[41] The committee simply reiterated its decision of 1660.[42] In the event a compromise was reached. In May 1690 Duppa deputed Harsnett together with Thomas Shirley to execute the orders of the House with an arrangement for sharing the resulting fees. On Harsnett's death in 1692 this function devolved on Shirley alone.[43]

Yeoman Usher

The office of yeoman usher of the parliament chamber was already in existence by the early 17th century when it appears to have been in the gift of the lord chamberlain of the household. In 1639 Charles Gedde was appointed to the post by lord chamberlain's warrant.[44] In 1661, however, John Whinyard, the then yeoman, stated that he was in waiting 'by a Warrant from the Lord High Chamberlain', presumably the lord great chamberlain.[45] In 1678 the crown granted the reversion of the office to Benjamin Cooling and his son Richard, successively, by letters patent under the great seal.[46] Whinyard died in November 1690. Under the terms of his patent Cooling could have claimed an unqualified right to succeed to the office. However, Duppa, 'In Consideracion of a Sum of Monyes then Paid him by Mr Benjamin Cooling', prevailed on the earl of Rochester to inform the house that 'It was the Right of the Black Rod to putt in a Yeoman Usher under him in the said Place'. Although a question was raised whether the office was in the gift of the lord great chamberlain, black rod carried his point and Cooling was duly admitted.[47] The matter was not definitely resolved until 1701 when, on the death of Cooling, the then black rod obtained a judgment in his favour against the surviving reversioner, Richard Cooling.[48]

---

[39] Royal Society, MS 70, pp. 62–3.

[40] Royal Society, MS 70, p. 91.

[41] Royal Society, MS 70, pp. 87–91.

[42] *LJ*, xiv, 375.

[43] Royal Society, MS 70, pp. 108–11.

[44] TNA, LC 5/134, p. 329.

[45] *LJ*, xi, 257.

[46] TNA, C 66/3202, no. 3.

[47] Royal Society, MS 70, pp. 99–101; *Manuscripts of the House of Lords*, new ser., iv, 146.

[48] *LJ*, xvii, 8.

Doorkeepers

The doorkeepers of the house of lords were appointed by black rod. By 1665 their number was fixed at eight sharing a sessional bounty paid by the treasury. Originally fixed at £100 this was reduced to £50 in 1685.[49] The doorkeepers' principal function was to assist black rod in maintaining order in the chamber and its surroundings. They also furnished the rooms of the great officers with the usual necessaries.[50]

Lord Chamberlain

The lord chamberlain of the household was in charge of the royal household 'above stairs'. Among his many responsibilities were the care and maintenance of the royal palaces. His relationship to the palace of Westminster differed from that of the other palaces in that he was subordinate to the lord great chamberlain from whom he received directions.[51]

The holders of the office who appear in this volume are the earls of Arlington 1674–85, Mulgrave 1685–8, Dorset 1689–97, Jersey 1700–4 and the duke of Shrews-bury 1710–15.

Earl Marshal

The earl of Surrey succeeded as 7th duke of Norfolk and as earl marshal in January 1684 and died in April 1701. He was evidently 'my Lord Duke' who officiated in the absence of the lord great chamberlain at the prorogation of 20 November 1685.[52] In February 1689 he ordered black rod to assist in the proclamation of William and Mary.[53]

---

[49] *CTB*, i, 646; vii, 177; viii, 491.
[50] Royal Society, MS 70, pp. Aiii–iv.
[51] Royal Society, MS 70, pp. 63–5.
[52] Royal Society, MS 70, p. 58.
[53] Royal Society, MS 70, p. 68.

The Text

Royal Society, London, MS 70

[p. 1]

Fees & Gratuities due and payable by the Right Honourable the Earl of Ossery for His Installation at Windsor[1]

	li	s	d
To the Dean of Windsor Register	34	13	04
To the Canon	6	13	04
To the Choir and Choristers	4	00	00
To the Verger and Choristers	1	10	00
To the Poor Knights	6	13	04
To the Register for a Book of Statutes	3	00	00
To the Dean towards Plate for the Altar	20	00	00
To the Garter Principall King at Arms for his Lordships Introduction and for Composition for his Upper Garment }	40	00	00
To him for his Fee	25	00	00
To the Gentleman Usher of the Black Rod	16	00	00
To the Officers of Arms	16	00	00
To all of them for Proclaiming his Lordships Stile	5	00	00
To the Wardrobe	2	00	00
To the Trumpetts	5	00	00
To the Serjeant Trumpiter	1	00	00
To the Musitians 4 Companies	6	00	00

[p. 2]

	li	s	d
To the Knight Harbinger	3	06	08
To the Drumms & Fifes	1	10	00
To the Porters	2	00	00
To the Master Cook	1	00	00
To the Serjeant Porter	1	00	00
To the Vestry	1	00	00
To the Yeomen & Harbingers	2	00	00
To the Ushers of the Hall	1	00	00
To the Grooms of the Chamber	1	00	00
To the Yeomen Usher	2	10	00

---

[1] Thomas Butler, styled earl of Ossory [I], installed as knight of the garter 25 Oct. 1672.

To the Quarter Wayters	3	06	00
To the Sewers	3	06	00
To the Buttery	1	00	00
To the Celler	1	00	00
To the Pantry	1	00	00
To the Serjeants at Armes	5	00	00
To the 12 Officers at Armes in lieu of Seats, Hatts & Feathers } for their Attendance at the Installation	20	00	00
To the Poor Knights given by my Lords Order	10	00	00
To the Serjeant Trumpet for Cap & Feathers 10 Guinees	10	15	00

Die

[p. 3]

Die Veneris 16 February 1676[2]

An Order for Attaching ye Duke of Buckingham[3]

> Ordered by the Lords Spiritual & Temporall in Parliament Assembled That the Gentleman Usher of the Black Rod Attending this House shall forthwith Attach the Person of George Duke of Buckingham, and bring him in safe Custody to the Bar of this House to morrow at Ten of the Clock in the Forenoon, this shall be a sufficient warrant in that behalf

John Browne[4] Clericus Parliamenti

To the Gentleman Usher of ye Black Rod Attending this house his Deputy & Deputys And to all Mayors Justices and others his Majestys Officers to be Ayding & Assisting in the Execution hereof.

Die Jovis 16 February 1670[5]

An Order for paying Proxy Fees to the Black Rod

> Upon reading the humble Peticion of Sir Edward Carteret[6] Gentleman Usher of the Black Rod Attending this House, shewing That he finds (among other things) there is a Fee of Thirty Shillings due to him from every Member of this House who sends in his Proxy, which hath not of late been paid, And for their Proxy's their Lordships directions therein. The

house

[p. 4]

> House being satisfied that this is such a Fee setled (among other things) in the Roll of Fees setled to be paid to the Officers Attending this House; As also a Fee of

[2] 1676/7; vacated 13 Nov. 1680. *LJ*, xiii, 42, 664.

[3] 2nd duke of Buckingham.

[4] See Appendix: Biographical Notes.

[5] 1670–1. *LJ*, xii, 431.

[6] See Appendix: Biographical Notes.

Ten shillings to the Yeoman Usher for every Proxy put in as aforesaid. It is this day Ordered by the Lords Spiritual and Temporall in Parliament Assembled, That the said Fees of 30s to the Gentleman Usher of the Black Rod, and 10s to the Yeoman Usher shall forthwith be paid; Together with the Fees usually paid to the Clerks by such lords as shall send in their Proxys to be Entred and Used upon Votes in this House

John Browne Clericus Parliamenti

Die Martis 3 Aprilis 1677[7]

An Order for Fees from ye Lords conveyed to the Tower by the Black Rod

Upon report made by the Earl of Ailesbury[8] for the Lords Committees for Privileges &c To whom was referred the Peticon of Sir Edward Carteret Gentleman Usher of the Black Rod; Praying that this house would Declare their Will and Pleasure before he demand any thing for Conveying Lords Committed by this House to his Maiestys Tower of London. That their Lordships find no direct President for Fees to the

usher

[p. 5]

Usher of the Black Rod for that Service, But being informed what Fees his Majestys Serjeants at Arms haue respectiuely received from time to time upon Carrying Noblemen to the seid Tower of London by Order of the King or Councell (viz From A Duke Twenty pounds, a Marquis Twenty Marks, an Earl Ten pounds, A Viscount Eight pounds, And a Baron Twenty Nobles; Are of Opinion that the Gentleman Usher of the Black Rod deserves as much at least, But their Lordships leaue the exact sum to the determinacon of this House. It is thereupon Ordered by their Lords Spiritual and Temporall in Parliament Assembled That there shall be respectiuely paid by ye Gentleman Usher of the Black Rod Attending this House for the time being, By a Duke Twenty pound; By a Marquis Twenty Marks; By an Earl Ten Pounds; By a Viscount Eight pounds; By a Baron twenty Nobles; Whenever the Black Rod shall Convey any Person of the said respectiue Degrees of Nobility to his Majestys Tower of London by Order of this House.

John Browne Clericus Parliamenti

Die

[p. 6]

Die Sabati 17 February 1676[9]

An Order for Conveying ye Duke of Buckingham to the Tower

Ordered by the lords Spirituall & Temporal in Parliament Assembled, That the Gentleman Usher of the Black Rod Attending this House shall take into his

---

[7] *LJ*, xiii, 97–8.

[8] 1st earl of Ailesbury.

[9] 1676/7; vacated 13 Nov. 1680. *LJ*, xiii, 39, 664.

Custody the Body of George Duke of Buckingham Member of this House, and him in safety to Convey to his Majesties Tower of London, for his high Contempt against this House, there to remain in safe Custody during his Majesties Pleasure, and the Pleasure of this House.

John Browne Clericus Parliamenti

To the Gentleman Usher of the Black Rod his Deputy and Deputys

17 February 1676[10]

Reciept Inde

Received then by the hands of Sir Edward Carteret Gentleman Usher of the Black Rod the Body of George Duke of Buckingham Prisoner.

John Robinson[11] Gentleman Gaoler

The Earl of Pembrokes[12] Commitment to the Black Rod
Die Martis 19 Martij 1677[13]
Order for commitment of the earl of Pembroke and Montgomery to the custody Sir Edward Carteret, black rod; signed John Browne, clerk of the parliaments

[p. 7]

The Kings Warrant to the Black Rod for Carrying my Lord of Pembroke to the Tower
Charles Rex
Whereas the Lords Spiritual & Temporall in Parliament Assembled, Did by their Order of the 19th March last, Committed Philip Earl of Pembroke

and

[p. 8]

and Montgomery to your Custody upon an Indictment of Murder brought against him, whereof he was found guilty before the Commissioners of Oyer and Terminer by the Grand Jury before them Impannelled. Our Will and pleasure is, That you Deliver the Person of the said Earl to Our Constable of our Tower of London, to be by him kept in safe Custody, till he shall be delivered by due Court of Law According to our Warrant directed to him in that behalfe. Which you shall herewith receive: And for soe doeing this shall be your Warrant. Given at our Court at Whitehall the first day of April 1678 in the 30th year of our reign.

By his Majesties Command
J Williamson[14]

To Our Trusty & Well beloued Sir Edward Carteret Knight Gentleman Usher of the Black Rod

[10] 1676/7.

[11] The gentleman gaolership of the Tower was distinct from that of the lieutenancy held by a different person although a namesake.

[12] 7th earl of Pembroke.

[13] 1677/8. *LJ*, xiii, 188.

[14] Sir Joseph Williamson, secretary of state. *ODNB*.

Receaved from Sir Edward Carteret Knight Gentleman Usher of the Black Rod the Body of the Right Honourable Earl of Pembroke and Montgomery by an Order under his Majestys hand and Signet this 2 day of April 1678

J Robinson

stationery

[p. 9]

Stationers Bill 10 October 1679

    To the Right Honourable the House of Peers Delivered to Sir Edward Carteret

2	large Frames filled with Wax Candles
2	Ream fine Horn folio Cutt
1	Bag of Sand
2	Leather Bottles of Inck
300	Dutch Pens
1	Pound of Perfumed Wax
1	Box of Dutch Wafers
4	Ream of fine horn folio cutt
6	large Standishes
2	Frames filled with Wax Candls
600	Dutch Pens
1	Pound of Perfumed Wax
1	Box of Wafers
3	Bottles of Inck
1	Bag of Sand
1	Dozen of Crimson Tape
1	Ream of Dutch Post Cutt
100	Dutch Quills
1	Bible richly bound
600	Dutch Pens
2	Frames filled with Wax Candles
4	Reams of Fine Horn
3	Reams of Fine Horn

2

[p. 10]

2	Frames filled with Wax Candles
2	Leather Bottles of Inck
2	Boxes of Wafers
400	Dutch Pens
2	Bundles of Wax Candles

Mr Mearnes[15] Bill for the House of Peers signed by me the 2nd of February 1680[16]

---

[15] Samuel Mearne, bookseller, bookbinder and stationer to the crown. *ODNB*.

[16] 1680/1.

An Order of my Lord Chamberlain[17] about Westminster Hall

These are to require you that you forthwith remove out of the Stage that was in Westminster Hall, Erected for the Tryal of my Lord Viscount Stafford and the other Lords in the Tower, All ye Woolpackes and Seates and other thing of Apparrelling on this Stage into some convenient place as you shall thinke safe till further occasion and this shall be your Warrant. Given under my hand this 23 January in the 32 year of his now Majesties Reign Annorum Domini 1680.[18]

To Sir Edward Carteret his Majesties Gentleman Usher of the Black Rod

13th October 1680

The Lord Great Chamberlains[19] letter about a Proxy

Sir

I am so powerfully seized upon

by

[p. 11]

by this generall New Feaver, that I find it impossible for me to giue my Attendances to his Majesty, according to my Intention at the opening of the Session, I desire therefore that you will take Care that the Houses be Searched according to the usual Custom, And as to the Introduction of the New Lords, I shall take it as a favour that my Lord Maynard[20] (if it be not inconvenient to his Lordship) may supply my Place.

Your Affectionate freind to serve you
Lindsey

To Sir Edward Carteret Gentleman Usher of the Black Rod

Sir Edward Carteret Instructions for Wayting on the House of Peers

For Mr Duppa

When you are sent by the King to the house of Commons, before there is a Speaker Chosen and Approved by the King, After your Three Leggs made, you must say Gentlemen of the House of Commons, The King commands this Honourable House to Attend him immediately in the House of Peers. If there be a Speaker, you must instead of Gentlemen of the House of

Commons

[p. 12]

Commons say Mr Speaker the King &c

When any Message comes from ye Commons to the Lords, you must acquaint my Lord Chancellor with it, and then goe to the Barr, And not call them in until my Lord Chancellor bids you.

---

[17] 1st earl of Arlington. See Appendix: Biographical Notes.

[18] 1680/1.

[19] 3rd earl of Lindsey. See Appendix: Biographical Notes.

[20] 2nd Baron Maynard

Coming in you must stand on the Right hand of him that brings the Message and make 3 Legs, and soe come to the Barr, but not before that my Lord Chancellor coms down to the Barr.

When there is a Message brought that requires an Answer, and the Messenger is called in, you must make 3 Legs, and soe come to the Bar, for my Lord Chancellor gives the Answer from the Woolsack.

When there is any Conference, you must give Order that all things be made ready, And when the Managers of the Conference are come you must acquaint the Lords with it.

When you come to Oxford and see that the Parliament is like to sitt there, Pray take me a Lodging with two good Beds, as cheap as you can

and

[p. 13]

and as neer the Parliament as you can, But if you perceiue they doe not sitt there, I leave it to your discretion. I shall leave the Keyes of all that is shutt up in Cubboards in the Parliament House, as also the Staff taken out of the Court in Westminster Hall with Mr Windham,[21] that lives in Bellyard in King street, who shall be ready to Wayte, and doe what is necessary. For Committees 6 Dozen Turky Workt Chaires, Candlestickes, Snuffers, Standishes the Stationers will furnish, with all other things. The Groom Porter will furnish all things that belong to him.

Fees due to the Gentleman Usher of the Black Rod for Entrances, &c.

Fees

The Prince for his first Entrance in to the Parliament House }	30:	00:	00:
An Archbishop	6:	13:	4
A Duke	10:	00:	00
A Marquess	6:	13:	4
An Earl	4:	10:	00
The Bishop of London, Durham & Winchester each of them }	3:	6:	8
A Bishop	2:	10:	00
A Viscount	4:	10:	00
A Baron	2:	10:	00

[p. 14]

All these are to be paid as well by those Lords who are newly Created, as by those to whom their Honours Descends

---

[21] Probably Mahaleel Windham, doorkeeper of the house of lords from 1674 until his death. Died 3 Feb. 1718, having 'been Door-Keeper to the House of Lords upwards of 40 years'. *Historical Register (Chronological Diary)* (1718), iii, 6.

And each Bishop Translated into another See, is to pay again according to the rates aforesaid

And also every Temporall Lord being created into a higher Honour, or to whom it descends is to pay again according to the Rates aforesaid

Every Lord is to pay for his Proxy Thirty Shillings

If any Lord newly Created send for his Proxy, he shall send also his Fees for his first Entrance into Parliament: till then his Proxy is not to be entered or allowed

Every Peer at the Ending of the Session giveth him freely, each Lord aboue a Viscount at least Two Pounds, Bishops and Barons One Pound

Fees

Fees dues to him by Bills

Every Private Bill at the first reading five Pounds More to him to provide Wine and Wafers for the Lords, Two Pounds If a Bill contain divers Persons

they

[p. 15]

they are to Pay for a Double Bill

Or if a Bill of Naturalizing containe many Persons, Each Person is pay soe much.

Fees due to him for Commitments

Every Peer committed into his Custody payes Twenty Nobles a Day

As for his Entertainment and all other Charges whatsoever, It is referred by him to the Nobleman's Discretion, who rewards him with Plate, or as he thinks fitt.

Every inferiour Person committed to him, payeth Ten Nobles, and for their Custody he hath every Day Ten Shillings.

If the person be in the Country, and is to be sent for, he payes yet more fees, each day Twenty shillings from the Beginning of the Parliament, and sending out of the writs to the rising thereof, he hath every day a Noble.

And if the Parliament be kept eleswhere then at Westminster, he hath allowance of Forty shillings as at the Parliament at Oxford.

As for his Majesties allowances for all necessaries belonging to the House, it is answered by the Officers upon demand, but he keepeth himself within

the

[p. 16]

the bounds of former Allowances, as thus

From the Woodyards, Coales allowed every day Two loads a day; Tallwood 2 loads a day; In the Winter time there is of Coales a week half a load more sent for.

And in the Summer time half allowance demanded

From the Chandry, Torches, Syzes, Wax Candles, & Tallow Candles are sent for as the House needeth.

From the Apothecary, Perfumes, Sweet Waters Urinals, & Earthen Potts.

From the Greate Wardrobe The King's Allowance of Sayes, of Canvas, of Wool, of Hair Thread, Lyar Nailes and other necessaries required for making ready the House[22] more then is imployed, so that the Remainder is demanded, or money taken for it, as also Hand Irons, Creepers, Forks, Tongs and Fireshovelles

The Surveyor is to give order to the Smith, whenever the Gentleman Usher requireth it, for Locks and Keyes, Hinges, Casements, Bolts and other Iron works as often as is needful.

The Printer upon demand is to answer

for

[p. 17]

for Paper, Inck, Pens, Standishes, Wax Penknifes, Service Bookes, Paper Bookes and other necessaries.

The Joyner upon demand is to furnish Tables, Formes, Joyntstooles, Cupboards, Tresells, where he appoints them to be placed, and soe many as he finds to be usefull.

The Removing Wardrobe is to send Close Stooles, Chamber Potts upon his demand, but these ought not to come from them but from the Great Wardrobe.

The Gentleman Usher of the Black Rods Fees for the Instalment of the Knights of the Order

The Prince One hundred Marks

A Duke Twenty Pounds

A Marquess Twenty five Marks

An Earl Twenty Marks

Three Cushions after their Instalment as his fee

The Lodge and little Park at Windsor belongs to him, as being appointed by the Order with the Meades thereunto belonging, the Hay is disposed by him.

The Deer being served he hath the

[p. 18]

keeping of 12 Milk Kine

The Vineyard also belongs to him

---

[22] For the provision of cloth and canvas for the house of lords on the eve of a session earlier see Alasdair Hawkyard and Maria Hayward, 'The Dressing and Trimming of the Parliament Chamber, 1509–58', *Parliamentary History*, xxix (2010), 229–37, particularly pp. 233–4.

He hath also Lodging within the Castle for which he had yearly Twenty Pounds but now doth lett it to his friend Mr Rosh[23] for Sixteen Pounds

He hath also for Fee Buck and Fee Doe

At the Arraignment of any of the Knights of the Order his Upper Robe belongs to him

When he sent sent beyond Sea to any Prince with Garter and an Order that he is to be imployed, his Allowance for Ordinary and Extraordinary is four Pounds a day

Chaires &c from the House of Peers to be sent to Oxford

Chaires & from the House of Peers to be sent to Oxford

These are to require you to cause the Turky Work Chairs, the Close Stools & Panns, Candlestickes and Chamberpotts that are in your Custody to be sent to Oxford for the use of the House of Peers there, And this shall be your Warrant Given under my hand the first day of March 1680 in the 33

[p. 19]

of his Majesties reign.[24]

Arlington[25]

To Sir Edward Carteret Knight Gentleman Usher of the Black Rod

Instructions   Instructions for Thomas Duppa Esquire When he waytes upon the Lords in Parliament the 14 August 1679

First you must desire my Lord Great Chamberlain or in his Absence he that Waits for him, to acquaint the Lords that the King hath appointed you to wait Black Rod in my Absence.

When he hath Acquainted their Lordships you must take the Black Rod in your Hand, and making Three Congees goo and star[26] at the Bar, and soe goe and sitt down a little while in the Black Rods Seat and putt up your Black Rod

You must suffer no Body to Walk thro' the House when the Lords are there

When the Lord Chancellor sitts in Westminster Hall, you must desire him to come up, when the Lords Command you, or the House is full or late.

[p. 20]

When my Lord Chancellor calls to cleer the House, you must see it to be done, and then shutt the Doors aboue the State;[27] The Yeoman Usher shut those below the Barr.

You must see that the Door Keepers keep the Painted Chamber, the Passages and the Lobby cleer.

[23] Possibly Dudley Rewse, receiver and paymaster general at Windsor Castle 1665–9. *HKW*, v, 478.

[24] 1 Mar. 1680/1.

[25] Lord chamberlain. See Appendix: Biographical Notes.

[26] *Sic*. May be 'stand'.

[27] The throne with all its fixtures and fittings.

When there is a Conference, the Painted Chamber and the Passages must be cleer, and you must pul open the New Gallery Door, That ye Members of the House of Commons may come in that way

Paper Pen and Inck must be putt before those that Grant the Conferences, but at a Free Conferenc of both sides the Table, and you must suffer none to come within the Bar but those that haue Right to be in the House when the House is sitting

You must take great Care that None Walk or make a Noyse when ther is a Conference.

When a Message comes from the House of Commons you must acquaint

my

[p. 21]

my Lord Chancellor with it, and then Stand upon the Step[28] at the Barr, until he bidds you call them in. And if you see that noe Lord is speaking, you may tell aloud at the Barr that there is a Message at the Door from the House of Commons.

When they are called in, you must take the Right Hand of him that brings in the Message, and standing a convenient distance from the Bar stay until my Lord Chancellor come to the Barr, and then making Three Leggs goe to the Barr with him that brings the Message If the Messengers be called in again to receive an Answer, then you must making your Three Congees come directly to the Barr.

When the King comes in his Robes, you must give notice of it to the Lords, and send your Doorkeepers to give them Notice, that they may have their Robes.

You must take Care both at Whitehall, and at the Parliament House that warning be given to every one

[p. 22]

that is to Attend upon the King when he comes in his Robes.

When the King is sett, either he or my Lord Great Chamberlain gives you Order to call the House of Commons. Then you goe immediately, and when you come there, you knock with the End of your Rod four or five times, and when the Doores are open, and come in as high as the Barr you make a Congee, and then going three steps further another, and then advancing further another And then holding up your Black Rod in your hand you say Mr Speaker, The King commands this Honourable House to Attend him immediately in the House of Peers. If there is no Speaker instead of Mr Speaker you say Gentlemen of this House of Commons, the King &c. Then you goe out making your Three Leggs, and stay for the Speaker in the Painted Chamber and going in, and standing at his

---

[28] The step was a low platform provided mainly for the speaker of the house of commons whenever he had to make an appearance in the upper House.

Right hand, not suffering any Body to stand betwixt him and you, you make three Congees, and goe and

stand

[p. 23]

stand with him at the Barr holding your Black Rod in your hand.

You must know when the House is adjourned to what time it is, and what Committees there are, that the Doorkeepers may attend, and he that does keep the Paper, Candles and other things. You are bound to attend at the Committee of Priviledges.

Triall of a Peer

The Manner of the Triall of a Peer

Upon Sunday morning April 30th 1666[29] Sir John Ayton Gentleman Usher of the Black Rod, with Garter King at Arms came to the Lord Chamberlain's lodgings. The Gentleman Usher brought a White Staff of about Eight foot long, being the Staff for the Lord High Steward.[30] And the Lord Chamberlain[31] carryed it into his Majesties Bedchamber. And the Lord Chamberlain delivered the Staff upon his Knee unto the King, and the King delivered the Staff unto the Gentleman Usher and Garter King at Armes[32] upon their Knees, and Commanded them to deliver it to the Lord High Steward.

Serjeants at Armes lye down on both sides the Stage.

[p. 24]

Gentlemen Usher and Black Rod, and the Warden of the Fleet, sitt in the Pitt before the Lord Steward.

The manner of Proceeding before the Lord High Steward

1.   Serjeants at Armes in Number 7

2dly.   The Purse Bearer went

3dly.   Black Rod with the Whitestaff – his Fee is £20

4ly.   Garter King at Armes

         Lord High Steward

         Mett upon Thursday ye 29th of June 1676

Thomas Duppa,[33] Esq, Black Rod in the Absence of Sir Edward Carteret, brought a White Rod of Nine foot long with Sir Edward Walker, Garter King at Armes unto my Lord Chamberlains Lodgings, who Carried them both to the King, and then took the Staff from the Gentleman Usher, And presented it to the

[29] Trial of 15th Baron Morley.

[30] 1st earl of Clarendon.

[31] 2nd earl of Manchester.

[32] Sir Edward Walker.

[33] See Appendix: Biographical Notes.

King upon his Knee. And then Garter and the Gentleman Usher kneeling, received the Staff from the Kings hand, with his Command to carry it to the Lord Chancellor Finch[34]

whom

[p. 25]

whom he had commissioned Lord High Steward of England, for the Tryall of the Lord Cornwallis[35] in Westminster Hall the 30th of June instant. This was done in the withdrawing Room to the Bedchamber at 11 a clock a little before the King went to the Chappell being St Peters Day.[36]

About 6 that Night I sent the Staff by my Man to be lodged till morning with Mr Hall my Lord's Gentleman Usher.

At 8 in the Morning June the 30th Sir Edward Walker and Mr Duppa went in a Coach to the Lord High Steward's house, and there attended till the Judges all came there, and after they and wee had all eaten Biskitts and drank burnt Claret, my Lord took Coach.

The White Staff was carried Erected in the Right Boot of the Coach, and Mace on the left, and Garter and the Purse in the Foreend of the Coach, Two Coaches of his Gentlemen went before, and all the Constables and Judges Coaches followed to Westminster Hall.

When Alighted

all

[p. 26]

All the Judges went into the Court before: then my Lord High Stewards Gentlemen and Officers: Then Six Serjeants with Maces: then Sir George Charnock[37] my Lords Mace and the Sheriff: Roger Harsnett[38] with a short White Staff: Then Garter King at Armes, and the Gentleman Usher with the White Staff. And next the Lord High Steward, who passed over the Court and took his Chair under the Cloth of State.

Garter and the Black Rod stood whilst the Court was called, and the Commission read, and then the White Staff was, presented by both upon their Knees: He rose up and received it, and then sat down in his Chair with it, and Paused, and then delivered it back to the Gentleman Usher, who took their places in the Court before the Lord High Steward, The Clerk of the Crown on the left hand, The White Staff held up all the time.

---

[34] Baron Finch of Daventry.

[35] 3rd Baron Cornwallis.

[36] 29 June.

[37] Serjeant at arms 1660–72; serjeant at arms to the lord chancellor 1673–84. *ORH*, i, 85.

[38] See Appendix: Biographical Notes.

The Sheriff and his White staff on the Right hand – Garter in his rich Coat. Then the serjeant

with

[p. 27]

with his Mace made the Oyes, and Proclaimed Silence – Then called the Lords of the Jury by Name, and so Proceeded to the Tryall.

Black Rod

> The Black Rods Reasons for his having the Apparrelling of the House of Lords in Westminster Hall at the Tryall of the Earl of Pembroke in April 1678. Which fees the Black Rod had.

Reasons and Proofes humbly Offered to the Consideration of the Right Honourable the Earl of Lindsey Lord Great Chamberlain of England by Sir Edward Carteret, Gentleman Usher of the Black Rod Clayming for his fees the Apparrelling of the house of Peers in Westminster Hall for the Tryall of the Right Honourable the Earl of Pembroke & Montgomery the 4th of April 1678.

Mr Maxwell a Servant to the Queen is ready to make Oath that he hath heard severall times Charles Gady[39] (who was Yeoman Usher and Secretary to Mr James Maxwell[40] Gentleman Usher of the Black Rod, his Unkle) and also Mery an

old

[p. 28]

Old Door-Keeper say, That the said Mr Maxwell the Black Rod, had all the Apparrelling within the House of Westminster Hall for his Fees at the Tryall of the Earl of Strafford.[41]

I can produce your Lordship an abstract of a Book of the Workes, under the hand of Inigo Jones[42] and Henry Wicks[43] that says that the Timber and materialls at the Tryall of the Earl of Strafford, were taken away by the Great Chamberlain & Gentleman Usher of the Black Rod to the late King upon pretence of Fees due to them.

James Turner[44] will take his Oath that Sir John Ayton Gentleman Usher of the Black Rod, had the Apparrelling of the House of Lords at Oxford for his Fees. He says moreover that he was a Servant to the Black Rod then, and One of the

---

[39] One Charles Gedde was appointed yeoman usher of the parliament house 23 Apr. 1639. TNA, LC 5/134, p. 329.

[40] See Appendix: Biographical Notes.

[41] Mar. 1641.

[42] Surveyor of the king's works 1615–40 or later. *HKW*, iii, 406.

[43] Paymaster of the king's works 1617–40 or later. *HKW*, iii, 407.

[44] Doorkeeper of the house of lords 1671–81. *CTB*, iii, 373; vii, 177.

Door-Keepers, and that he hath still a Wast coat made out of the Stuff of the said Fees, which his Master gave him. He doth

also

[p. 29]

also tell me that Calender,[45] Noble,[46] and Safe,[47] can Witness that the Black Rod had the said Apparrelling Fees at Oxford

Mr Whiniard[48] can justifie, if your Lordship be pleased to ask him, That Mr Thanes,[49] Sir John Ayton,[50] and my Self, have without the least Question in the World quietly enjoyed to this day, all the Apparelling of what kind soever that belongs to the House of Peers, and that doth not returne to the Kings Wardrobe. It is alsoe to be Considered that the whole Furniture and all other things whatsoever of the House of Peers in Parliament is under the Charge and Care of the Black Rod, and if anything is lost or spoyled he is to pay for it, And therefore doth very well deserve those small Fees that he hath.

The King's Warrant for Apparreling the Court in Westminster Hall to the Master of the Great Wardrobe doth Direct him to Deliver or cause to be delivered the severall parcells

[p. 30]

therein conteyned to Sir Edward Carteret Gentleman Usher of the Black Rod, for which he must give them of the Great Wardrobe a Receipt, for untill then they cannot Pass it on Account, nor be paid for. The Black Rod giving such a Receipt the parcells must be delivered to him, and be his Fees when no more fitt for the Kings Service, Or else he is used worse then any Officer in the Kings house, which he can never think of soe great an Officer as your Lordship is, And hope having served the King about 30 years, he shall not be worse in this particular then any of his Predecessors of Fellow Servants.

When the Officers of the Wardrobe at Whitehall have any Stuff delivered to them to Cover any Scaffolds or Boards both the Board and Stuff is their Fees, as far as it is covered, and there is a Composition betwixt the Officers of the Workes and them for the said Fee

That

---

[45] Archibald Callender, doorkeeper of the house of lords 1665–78. *CTB*, i, 646; vii, 177.

[46] James Noble, doorkeeper of the house of lords 1665–85. *CTB*, i, 646; viii, 491.

[47] Thomas Safe, a servant of the groom porter 1662–7. TNA, AO 3/131, f. 29.

[48] John Whiniard, housekeeper of the house of lords 1635–90, yeoman usher 1660–90. Died 7 Nov. 1690. J.C. Sainty, 'The Office of Housekeeper of the House of Lords', *Parliamentary History*, xxvii (2008), 256–60; *LJ*, xi, 257.

[49] Probably Alexander Thayne appointed black rod 1642. Served the house of lords until 1649. Attempted to recover the office after the Restoration but despite his appearance on 9 July 1660 (see below, p. 41), he was unable to secure it in the event. E. Ashmole, *The Institution, Laws and Ceremonies of the Most Noble Order of the Garter* (1672), 256–7.

[50] See Appendix: Biographical Notes.

[p. 31]

That the same Person hath not the Scaffolding and Apparrelling for his Fee is evident, For at the King's Coronation The Dean and Prebends of Westminster had almost all the Apparrelling, The Baron of the Cinque Ports[51] had some, And the Kings Gentleman Ushers had the Cloth of Gold upon which the Chair of State stood, of which I have my share still to shew. And I am in formed that my Lord Great Chamberlain had all the Clothes & Robes that the King wore that day.

All these reasons and Presidents will Induce (I hope) My Lord Great Chamberlain to let me quietly & with his favour enjoy the said Fees which my Predecessors Black Rods have always enjoyed, having to the utmost of my power performed the Duty of my Place, with as much Care and diligence as any of them ever did. And that his Lordship will be pleased to consider that the

great

[p. 32]

great trouble and paines and some charge too that I have been at in procuring the Warrants and getting the said Court apparelled and in saving the Stuff after the Tryall was over does not only deserve the said Fees (which in themselves are very in considerable) but some share in those great advantages which have been made by the Scaffolds. Having also the honour to be the immediate Officer to your Lordship in the house of Peers where I did undergo a long and tedious Duty the day of the Tryal.

All this I leave to your Lordships consideration humbly begging your favour & kindness which I doe value aboue these or any other fees whatsoever.

> A Warrant to Deliver to the Black Rod from the Great Wardrobe what is necessary for Apparelling the House of Lords at the Tryall of the Earl of Strafford

Parliament Provision against the Tryall of the earl of Strafford[52]

Great Wardrobe To be delivered to Mr Maxwell Gentleman Usher of the Black Rod[53]

> A Warrant to Samuel Pindar Esquire Clerk of the Robes for the drawing up of a Warrant for the Kings hand directed to the Master of the Great Wardrobe[54] for the delivery of the parcell following unto James Maxwell

Esquire

[p. 33]

Esquire Gentleman Usher of the Parliament for the making ready the Great Hall at Westminster against the Tryall of the Earl of Strafford (Viz) 22 Pieces of Say of

---

[51] *Sic.* Presumably plural in the master copy.

[52] Marginalia written in a different hand from the rest of the text.

[53] Marginalia written in a different hand from the rest of the text.

[54] Earl of Montagu. See Appendix: Biographical Notes.

the largest Size, 160 Ells of Canvas to make Sacks, and to Cover Stooles and Formes 12 Todd of Wool for stuffing all the Stools & Formes within the Hall, wich are appointed for the Lords, and to pay for the Hay to fill the Sacks and to provide Threed, Lyars Nails and pay for the Workmanship of all the premisses and to furnish whatelse shall be needfull for this Service with all possible speed.

Memorandum these are the same allowances which are usually made for the Parliament House.

Painted Chamber orders to be observed there[55]

An Order &c to keep the Footmen &c out of the Painted Chamber
Die Jovis 30 May 1678[56]

Upon report made this day by the Lord Privy Seal[57] from the Lords Committees appointed to consider of the Priviledges of the House of Peers, as concerning the means of ye keeping good order in the painted Chamber and the Passages & Lobbys belonging to the House of Peers

[p. 34]

that their Lordships have perused the former Orders of the House made in the like Case and doe find that the Case of keeping good Order in those places belongeth to the Charge of the Gentleman Usher of the Black Rod Attending this House, together with the Yeoman Usher and other Under Officers and Door Keepers.

Upon consideration had thereof It is Ordered By the Lords Spiritual and Temporal in Parliament Assembled That the Painted Chamber and the Lobby between it and the House of Peers shall by the Care of the said Gentleman Usher of the Black Rod the Yeoman Usher and the Door Keepers be kept clear from all Footmen and all other Persons not having business with the Lords (except such Gentlemen and Pages as Attend the Lords and their Assistants) And that no Person unless such as haue Occasion to speak with some Peer, be admitted further then the Painted Chamber. And also that the Knight Marshalls Men appointed to Attend the House do take Care to keep the Staires and Avenues to the House of Peers and also the Court of Requests cleer from all disturbances by Footmen or any other

person

[p. 35]

Persons. And it is furthered Ordered That the Lord Great Chamberlain be, and is hereby desired to take Care, givis charge to the said Gentleman usher and yeoman Usher and their under officers and door Keepers As also to the Knight Marshalls Men respectiuely to see that these orders be duly observed And that the Orders relating to the Painted Chamber Lobbys Court of Request and Staires be fixed to Doores belonging to this House, that all Persons may take Note thereof. And lastly It is Ordered that his Majesty may be desired from the house or my Lord

---

[55] Marginalia written in a different hand from the rest of the text.

[56] *LJ*, xiii, 233.

[57] 1st earl of Anglesey.

Great Chamberlain, That a Canopy of State may be sett up in the Little Committee Chamber as heretofore hath been accustomed.

John Browne Clericus Parliamenti

Deputy or Assistant to Sir John Ayton Black Rod[58]

The Kings Letter to Sir John Ayton for the Surrender of ye Black Rod

Upon the humble suit and Request of our Trusty and well beloved Servant Sir John Ayton our Gentleman Usher of the Black Rod. We are pleased in Consideration of his Great Age and long and faithfull Attendance upon our Person, and for the

[p. 36]

better performance of our Service to Grant unto him One Deputy and Assistant in the Attendance upon the House of Peers in Parliament and elsewhere And therefore our Will and Pleasure is and wee doe by these presents Authorise constitute and appoint our Trusty and well beloved Servant Sir Edward Carteret one of our Gentlemen Ushers Dayly Wayters to Execute and perform the said Service in his Absence. Given at our Palace at Whitehall the 28th day of May 1661.

An Order for Keeping out of People when the King cometh in his Robes to the house of Peers.

Die Sabati 17° Februarij 1676[59]

This House taking Notice of the great disorders and Inconveniences which have sundry times hapned in this Place, by reason of the great Numbers of People coming into and remaining within the Dores thereof, at such tims as his Majesty hath Appointed to come publickly to this House, to speak to both Houses of Parliament, Or give his Royal Assent to Bills. By reason whereof the Lords have been soe Crowded, that they have not had room to come to, or abide in

their

[p. 37]

their places in the said House, which hath been to the great disturbances of such solemn Meetings. It is this day therefore Ordered By the Lords Spiritual and Temporall in Parliament Assembled, for prevention of the like disorders and inconveniences for the future, That the Lord Great Chamberlain of England be, & his Lordship is his hereby Desired to take Care and give such Orders for their Keeping Shutt of all the Doores belonging to the House of Peers at such solemn times. So that no Person whatsoever except the Members of the House and their Assistants and the Eldest Sons of Noblemen and the Officers and Attendants of, and belonging to the said House, be suffered to come into and remain within the Doores thereof

John Browne Clericus Parliamenti

Aaron Smith committed to the Black Rod

[58] Written in a different hand from the rest of the text.
[59] 1676/7. *LJ*, xiii, 44.

Die Martis 5° Martij 1677[60]

Order for commitment of Aaron Smith to the custody of Sir Edward Carteret, black rod; signed by John Browne, clerk of the parliaments

[p. 38]

Mr Smiths Fees

Fees due upon the Discharge of Mr Aaron Smith to the officers of the House of Peers.

	l	s	d
To the Clerk of the Parliament	3	6	8
To the Clerk Assistant	1	0	0
For the Order of Discharge & reading the Peticion	0	16	6
	£5	3	2
To the Gentleman Usher of the Black Rod	3	6	8
To ye Yeoman Usher	1	0	0
Total	£9	9	10

Sir Edward Carteret Black Rods Pencion 200li per annum

A Copy of the Dormant Warrant of Sir Edward Carteret being the Pencion of Two hundred pounds per annum

After our hearty Commendacons By Virtue of his Majesties letters Patents Granting ye Annuity or yearly Pencion of Two hundred Pounds to Sir Edward Carteret Knight Upon which it appears by your Certificate bearing date the 28 April last, to be One hundred Pounds due for

half

[p. 39]

half a year ended at our Lady day last 1679 These are to Pray and require to make and pass Debentures or Draw orders from time to time for what is already due, and shall hereafter from time to time grow due to the said Sir Edward Carteret or his Assigns upon the said Pencion and let the same be satisfied out of any his Majesties Tresaure now or at any time hereafter being and remaining in the Receipt of the Exchequer. And for soe doing this shall be your Warrant. Whitehall Treasury Chamber May 3. 1679

Essex[61]
L. Hyde[62]
J. Ernle[63]
Ed. Deering[64]
S. Godolphin

[60] 1677/8. *LJ*, xiii, 172.

[61] 1st earl of Essex.

[62] Laurence Hyde, later 1st earl of Rochester. See Appendix: Biographical Notes.

[63] Sir John Ernle. *HPC, 1660–1690*, ii, 271–4.

[64] Sir Edward Dering, 2nd bt. *HPC, 1660–1690*, ii, 208–14.

To our very Loving Friend Sir Robert Howard Knight[65] Auditor of the Receipt of his Majesties Exchequer

Allowances of Wood, coal at King Charles Funeral 1684[66]

Delivered for the Princes Lodging & Lords house the 12. 13. & 14th February 1684

Charcoal 6 Quarters per diem

Scullery

Delivered for the Princes Lodgings & Lords house the 12. 13. & 14th February 1684

Billets   5 ⎫
Tallwood iiij load ⎬ per Diem

Woodyard

Delivered for the Service of the Lords Committee sitting in the Painted Chamber at

[p. 40]

Westminster to begin the 23th of March 1684/5 and to continue till further Order

Faggotts   iiij ⎫
Scotch Coals   cc ⎬ per Diem

to the Woodyard

Commission for Deputy Black Rod

    The Forms of the Commission given to Mr Duppa per Boreman[67] to be Deputy Black Rod

Charles by the Grace of God King of England Scotland France and Ireland Defender of ye faith & Soveraigne of the most Noble Order of the Garter. Whereas out of our special regard to the Honourable House of Peers, And it hath been the Will and Pleasure of our Royall Predecessors to Appoint the Usher of the Black Rod one of the Officers of our most Noble House of Peers, and to be subservient to them during their Sitting in Parliament And because there is a necessity of One to perform allways that Duty, And that Sir Edward Carteret may be either Absent or hindered by sickness from that service Wee at his request and for the better performances of that Duty and Service which we would have

rendered

---

[65] See *ODNB*; *HPC, 1660–1690*, ii, 595–604.

[66] 1684/5.

[67] Thomas Boreman. A member of the family based at Greenwich, and employed in a variety of posts connected with the royal household. Sir William Boreman (*d.* 1686), its most prominent figure, who ended his career as second clerk of the greencloth, was appointed administrator of his goods after his death in 1678–9. Keeper of game, Greenwich Park 1667–78; under-housekeeper, Greenwich Palace 1670–4 or later; keeper of the Queen's House, Greenwich 1671; ?gentleman usher daily waiter by 1675. *CTB*, vi, 309, 311; TNA, LC3/24, rot. 12.

[p. 41]

rendered to that Honourable Assembly are graciously pleased to Name and Appoint our Trusty and well beloved Servant Thomas Boreman[68] esquire One of our Gentlemen Ushers Dayly Wayters to be Ayding and Assisting unto the said Sir Edward Carteret in discharge of the said Attendance upon the House Peers as such times and upon such Occasions as thro' his Indisposition, infirmity or other Imployments about our Service the said Sir Edward Carteret shall not find himself of Sufficient Ability to perform the same. Given at our Court at Whitehall Under the Signet of our said Order the day of [blank] in the 27th year of our Reign 1675.

> To the Right Honourable the Lords Commissioners Knights of the most Noble order of the Garter
> The humble Peticion of Sir Edward Carteret Knight Gentleman Usher of the Black Rod

Humbly Sheweth.

> That the King Soveraign of the most Noble Order of the Garter hath been graciously Pleased to Grant unto your Person The Office of Gentleman Usher of the Black Rod with all Privileges Proffits Perquisites & advantages thereto

[p. 42]

belonging in as ample a manner as any ever enjoyed it at any time.

That there has lately been given to him a Lyst of Fees due to him as Black Rod found in the Chest and amongst ye Writings of James Maxwell Esquire Black Rod. In which List he finds that the Custody of the Knights of the Garter after the Installment are his Fees But so it is may it please ye Lordships That the late Register and Garter taking advantage of the ignorance in those things of ye Peticioner did defraud him of the said Cushions

> Wherefore he Doth most humbly Pray your Lordshipps the premises considered to Order the said Cushions to be delivered to him as a Fee justly belonging to his Office of Black Rod

---

[68] This is the only reference to Thomas Boreman's appointment as a gentleman usher daily waiter so far discovered (2014). His name does not appear in the far from complete records of the gentlemen ushers from the reign of Charles II (TNA, LC3). In particular, his name does not occur in the cheque roll for the king's servants (TNA, LC3/24, rots 7, 8). Under gentlemen ushers quarter waiters there appear two men with a surname (Bowman) not unlike Boreman. Both Edward Bowman and Francis Bowman were sworn on 11 June 1660. On 30 Aug. 1679 Edward Bowman was said to be dead and two days later he was replaced by Charles Richards. On Francis Bowman surrendering his appointment he was succeeded by Jeremiah Bubb on 1 June 1674; Francis Bowman died some time before 1685 (TNA, LC3/24, rots 7, 8). Thus, neither of the Bowmans can be identified with the man being named deputy black rod in regnal year 27 Charles II, that is, 30 Jan. 1675–30 Jan. 1676. In the cheque roll under Greenwich the entry for the under-keeper of the palace is 'dead John Boreman Esq sworne . . . Apr. 23: 1674' (TNA, LC3/24, rot. 12). In their contracted forms John and Thomas are similar, and have frequently been confused: in this case the entry for the under-keeper should have been Thomas Boreman. Thus, we know that the under-keeper was alive a year before the commission for deputy black rod was drafted, but he was dead by 1679 (*CTB*, vi, 309, 311). This creates a presumption that Thomas Boreman, the under-keeeper at Greenwich, was designated a gentleman usher daily waiter – and intended for deputy to black rod – but for some reason unknown his designation did not proceed, and he was never sworn. The man who then became deputy black rod was another gentleman usher, Thomas Duppa.

And he shall Pray &c

An Account of Furniture for ye Parliament House April ye first 1685 against the Coronacion And the sitting of the Peers

3   Dozen of Turky Work Chaires for Committees
1   Dozen in the Lord Great Chamberlains Lodgings
1   Dozen in the Lord Treasurers Lodgings

[p. 43]

1   Dozen in the Lord Keepers Lodgings
1   Red Cloth Cushion for the Bishop to kneel upon that reads Prayers to ye house of Lords
A   New Clock with a fair Dyall and a Box for the Lords to run in
9   Great Pewter Candlesticks and 4 pair of Snuffers for the House of Peers & Princes Lodgings to be allways ready
6   Lesser Candlestickes and 4 pair of Snuffers for the Lord Archbishop, the Lord Chancellor & Lord Treasurers Roomes
4   Large pewter Candlesticks and 1 pair of Snuffers for the Painted Chamber
9   Close stools with double Pans
9   Chamber potts for all the Rooms
22   Pieces of Say of the longest Size to Cover the Woolpacks Formes & Benches
160 Ells of Canvas to make Sacks and Cover Stooles and Formes
12   Tod of Wool for stuffing all the Formes and Stooles which are appointed for the Lords – likewise Hay for the said Sacks
     For Thread Lyars and Nailes
     For to cover the two Seates on both sides the State[69] with Crimson Velvet to be
     Nailed down with Silver & Gold Galoon Lace
     As much green Serge as will hang the Lord

[p. 44]

Archbishops of Canterburys Roomes, the Lord Chancellors Rome and the Lord Treasurers Roome, and the Lord Great Chamberlains Room

The Lobby adjoyning to the Princes Lodgings to be hung with Green Bayes and under the Window

The Kings Stool Roome to be hung and furnished by the Wardrobe

The Princes Lodgings to be hung by ye Wardrobe and new Matted by Mr Surveyours[70] Order and the Kings Stool Room to be made ready there

A Note of what goods are to be provided for the Lords House for the Coronacion & Parliament.

To Thomas Neale,[71] Esquire, his Majesties Groom Porter

Sir   You are desired to Provide and send in to me against the 23th of this instant April 1685 for the Coronacion of his Majesty King James the Second

---

[69] The throne with its steps, hangings and canopy.
[70] Sir Christopher Wren, surveyor-general of the king's works. *HKW*, v, 469.
[71] See *HPC 1660–1690*, iii, 129–31; *ODNB*.

which Goods are also to serve for the use of the Lords House &c against the next Sitting of Parliament appointed the 19 of May next These particulars following

[p. 45]

1	Iron Grate for fire where his Majesty changeth his Robes in the Abby of Westminster
6	Spanish Tables
6	Sconces of Brass
6	Wall Plates
2	Great Lanthorns
6	half Lanthorns
4	Pair of Bellowes
6	Pair of Snuffers
1	Pair of Great Brass Andirons
1	Pair of Strong Andirons for Log Wood with a great Fireshovell and Tongs for the Lords House
6	Pair of Small Andirons and 6 pair of Tongs for several other Rooms there.

Examined by Thomas Duppa Black Rod

Court of Claymes

1st Memorandum A Court of Claymes was Provided at the Charge of the King James the 2d. By the Officers of the Great Wardrobe in the Painted Chamber at the Parliament House. The Tables and Formes were all Covered with Green Bayes, and 12 Green Cloth Cushions fringed new were sett behind the Table in the Windowes but not used. This Court

[p. 46]

consisted of Twenty five of the Greatest Officers and Peers of his Majesties House and Courts of Westminster. The Lord Keeper[72] was Chief which held about Eight several Dayes to receive all Peticions in French for what Duty each Person was obliged to doe Services at the Coronacion of the King By which they Claimed by the Holding of severall Tenures of Lands and Mannors in several Counties of England And what particular Fees each Person Claymed and was Allowed at the last

4[73]   Coronation of the King Charles the Second

The Gentlemen Ushers

Found at time That by their Peticion then presented for severall Services Ordered them by Warrant from the Lord Chamberlain they were to take care and see that several Scaffolds and Rayles and two pair of Staires and Two Thrones were Erected in St Peters Church in Westminster or in the Place the King and Queen

---

[72] 1st Baron Guilford.

[73] *Sic.*

should be Crowned, and that the Traverses were made in St Edwards Chappell And that the said Thrones were covered with Cloth of Gold and Red Sarge and

Mats

[p. 47]

Matts under them. And that they had allwayes had for their Fees the Serges that covered the said Thrones and Stepps.

Die Sabati 22° Junij 1678[74]

Order to Sir Edward Carteret, black rod, to convey Gerard Herbert to the prison of the Fleet

[p. 48]

Aprilij 28th 1685

Whereas his Majestie hath been graciously Pleased to give unto Sir Thomas Duppa Knight First Gentleman Usher Dayly Wayter and Black Rod, Charles Cotterell[75] Esquire Henry Carr[76] Esquire Bryan Turner[77] Esquire his Majestys Gentleman Ushers Dayly Wayters The Cloth of Gold or of Tissue which Covered the Throne in Westminster Abby at his Majesties Coronacion as a Reward for their Services and Duty on that day as it had been given at the Coronacion of his late Majesty of blessed Memory unto their Predecessors. These are therefore to require you to deliver unto them the Cloth of Gold or Tissue which Covered the King and Queens Thrones and for soe doeing this shall be ye Warrant. Given under my hand this 28 day of April 1685 in the first year of his Majesties Reign

Arlington

To Philip Kinnersley esquire Yeoman of the Removing Wardrobe

At the Court at Whitehall ye 3d of April 1685

It is this day ordered by his Majesty in Council that the Right Honourable the Earl

of

[p. 49]

of Arlington Lord Chamberlain of his Majesties Household doe Appoint Persons to wait at the Lords Tables and other Great Tables at the Coronacion

Philip Musgraue[78]

April 17th 1685

My Lord

I haue enclosed sent to your Lordshp a Note of some things that are to be furnished in the Abby Church and Westminster Hall against the day of his Majesties Coronacion. And because I might make an Omission by giving your

---

[74] *LJ*, xiii, 258.

[75] An error for Carteret; gentleman usher daily waiter 1685–8. TNA, LC 3/56, p. 22; *ORH*, i, 83.

[76] Gentleman usher daily waiter 1680–8. *ORH*, i, 83.

[77] Gentleman usher daily waiter 1682–8. *ORH*, i, 178.

[78] Clerk of the privy council 1684–9. *HPC, 1660–1690*, iii, 120.

Sir Thomas Duppa as gentleman usher of black rod marked G, accompanied by Windsor herald marked H and the lord mayor of London marked I, walks in the coronation procession of James II towards the end of the section immediately following the king. British Museum, Prints and Drawings, 1849,0315.124 © Trustees of the British Museum.

Lordship an Account but of some particulars I desire your Lordship will take care that all the Works done upon the Kings Account both in the Abby Church and Westminster Hall may be furnished with all things necessary and suitable to so great a Solemnity. I am

Your Lordships most humble servant

Lindsey

A lyst of his Majesties Servants Ordered to Attend in the Hall & Abby at the Coronacion of King James and Queen Mary the 23th of April 1685

[p. 50]

1	The Gentleman Usher of the Black Rod and 2 Servants	3
2	Three other Gentlemen Ushers to Attend ij tables in the Hal	3
3	Nine Sewers for Nine Messes	9
4	Six Pages and Groomes to Attend ye Lords at the Kings Table	6
5	Six at the inside and 6 more Wayteres on the Outside of the Lord & Ladies Tables	12
6	Twelve more at the Judges Barons of the Cinque Ports and the Kings Councell at Law	12
7	Six Wayters more at the Lord Major and Aldermen	6
8	Six more to Attend the Kings Heralds &c	6

Sir Thomas Duppa Mr Windham and Henry Griffith Charles Cotterell[79] Henry Carr & Bryan Turner Esquire Sir Edward Carteret[80] Mr Luring Sir Richard Brown[81] John Thomas[82] Esquire Jeremy Bubb[83] Jeremy Chaplain[84] Charles Richards[85] Robert Peterman Esquire James Gibbons[86] Esquire for ye Sewer

Mr

[p. 51]

Mr Woodhouse Mr Hopkins Mr [blank] 4 Pages
Mathew Windham Henry Griffith to help them

These are to Will and require you forthwith upon sight hereof to provide & proceed to finish a convenient Room over the Passage leading to the House of Offices belong to the Lords house of Parliament according to such directions as you shall receive from the Gentleman Usher of the Black Rod Attending that House for the better keeping and securing of such prisoners as shall at any time be committees to his Custody. And also for keeping and preserving of Pens Inck Paper Wax and all sorts of Candlestickes and lights for the use of the Lords at Committees in the House of Peers and in the Princes Lodgings and Painted Chamber as need requires And for soe doeing this shall be your Warrant dated the [blank] day of May in the first year of the Reign of our Soveraign Lord King James the Second of England Scotland France and Ireland Defender of the Faith &c Anno Domini 1685

Lindsey

To Sir Christopher Wren Knight Surveyor of the his Majesties Works

---

[79] An error for Carteret as above, Note 75.
[80] Probably cupbearer 1685–8. *ORH*, i, 83.
[81] Probably 2nd bt, carver 1685–9. *ORH*, i, 78.
[82] Probably gentleman sewer 1685–9. *ORH*, i, 78.
[83] Gentleman usher quarterly waiter 1674–89. *ORH*, i, 79. See also *HPC 1660–1690*, i, 74–1.
[84] Probably gentleman usher quarterly waiter 1677–92. *ORH*, i, 79.
[85] Probably gentleman usher quarterly waiter 1683–5. *ORH*, i, 153.
[86] Probably clerk of the robes and wardrobes 1685–9. *ORH*, i, 109.

[p. 52]

An Order to Invest Thomas Duppa Esquire in the Office of Black Rod At a Chapter of the Garter held at Windsor the 6th of May 1683. There being Present the Soveraign. His Royal Highness the Duke of York The Duke of Ormond The Earl of Oxford The Duke of Beaufort[87] The Earl of Arlington The Duke of Grafton and the Duke of [blank]

Being all. And Dr Fulham the Senior Prebend then Deputy to the Dean of Windsor Register (The Dean being absent and Sick) and Garter vested in their Mantles. Entred the Chapter house Garter carrying a Mantle whereon lay the Gold Chains and Badge belonging to the Usher of the Black Rod hanging thereat. As also the Black Rod & Patten under the Great Seals of the Order for constituting Thomas Duppa Esquire [(]One of his Majesties Gentlemen Ushers Dayly Wayters) Usher of the Black Rod in the Room of Sir Edward Carteret Knight deceased The said Mr Duppa following them

Being come to the lower End of the Table they all made their Obeysance

the

[p. 53]

the like also in the Middway and when they came neer the Soveraign

This done, Garter kneeling down Presented the Patten to his Majesty who delivering it to the Deputy Register he read it & returned it back to his Majesty who gaue it to Mr Duppa.

Then Garter by the Soveraigns Command put the Mantle on Mr Duppa who kneeling down his Majesty put the gold Chain about his Neck and delivered the Black Rod into his hands.

Lastly Mr Duppa still kneeling, & laying his hand upon a Bible the Deputy Register read the Oath usually taken by the Usher of the Black Rod Whereupon Mr Duppa kissing the Book The Soveraign Drew his Sword and Knighted him which done he kissed the Kings hand and rose up.

All which being performed the Soveraign and the Knights Companions putting off their Mantles departed.

The Oath to be administred by his Majesties Gentlemen Usher Dayly Wayters to his Majestys Servants of the Bedchamber

You shall swear on the holy Evangelist[88] and by the Contents of this Book And

[p. 54]

by the faith you bear unto Almighty God to be a true Servant unto our Soveraign Lord James by the Grace of God King of England Scotland France and Ireland Defender of the Faith &c you shall know nothing that be any wayes hurtfull or prejudiciall to the King's Majestys Royall Person State Crown or Dignity but you

[87] 1st duke of Beaufort.

[88] *Sic.*

shall hinder it what in you lyes or else reveal the same with all convenient Speed to the King of some of his Majestys most Honoble Privy Councill.

You shall serve the King truly and faithfully in the place where unto you are called as one of the [blank] of his Majesties Bedchamber in Ordinary to his Majesty.

You shall be obedient to the Lord Chamberlain &c in his Majesties Service out of the districts of the Bed Chamberlain.

So help you God and the Contents of this Book

Gentlemen, Pages Closet Keeper   Arlington

Barbers Laundress &c

[p. 55]

A Warrant for a Badge of Gold & Chain for Mr Duppa

These are to signify unto you their Majestys Pleasure that you prepare & deliver unto Thomas Duppa Esquire Gentleman Usher of the Black Rod A Chain of Gold and a Badge of Gold both Weighing Ten Ounces or thereabouts the Badge to be of the same fashion as is worn by the Gentleman Usher of the Black Rod And for soe doeing this shall be your Warrant Given under my hand this 12 day of March 1682/3 in the 31st year[89] of his Majestys Reign

Arlington

Whitehall Treasury Chamber

29th March 1683[90]

These are to require you to deliver to Sir Thomas Duppa Knight Gentleman Usher Dayly Wayter Black Rod for his Majestys Service at the House of Peers Four Ounces of Parfumes to burn and Two Bottles of Sweet Water to be allowed weekly during the Sessions of Parliament And for soe doeing this shall bee your Warrant Given under my hand this 17th of November 1683 in the first year of his Majestys Reign.[91]

Mulgrave[92]

To James St Amand[93] Esquire

and

[p. 56]

And James Chate[94] Esquires Apothecaries to his Majestys Royall Person their respective Waytings

[89] An error for 35th.

[90] This entry purports to give treasury approval to the execution of a warrant, but the warrant which follows is dated 17 Nov. 1683, that is, more than seven months later.

[91] The dating of this entry is erroneous. The year should be not 1683 but 1685, that is, the first year of James II's reign. This is corroborated by the fact that Mulgrave, in whose name the warrant was issued, did not become lord chamberlain until Oct. 1685.

[92] 3rd earl of Mulgrave. See Appendix: Biographical Notes.

[93] Joint apothecary to the person 1685–8. *ORH*, i, 162. See also *HPC 1660–1690*, iii, 379–80.

[94] Chase. Joint apothecary to the person 1685–8. *ORH*, i, 85.

Let this Warrant be Executed
    Rochester
    J Ernle
    Ed Deering
    S Godolphin

These are to Authorise and Appoint you to take off all the Green Cloth & Serge with other small Materials thereunto belonging that Covers the Court which was erected for the Tryall of the Lord Delamer[95] in Westminster Hall and secure them till you shall receive Orders from me And this shall be your Warrant. Given under my hand this 15th day of January 1685.[96]

Lindsey

To James Serjeant Upholsterer in Westminster
For the Gentleman Usher of ye Black Rod

These are to require you and every of you to be Attendant on Thursday the 14th of this Instant January at the Court then to be held in Westminster for the Tryall of the right Honourable the Lord Delamer to doe your Duties in Keeping

the

[p. 57]

the Doores and Passages in and neer the said Court and to obey such further Orders as you shal receive from me Given under my hand the 8th day of January 1685

Lindsey

To James Noble &c the rest of the Doorkeepers of the House of Peers
January 15th 1685[97]

My Lord[98]

I humbly acknowledge your Lordships favour and Bounty to me in bestowing on me the Apparelling of the Scaffold erected for the Tryall of the Right Honourable Lord Delamer in Westminster Hall which I receive from your Lordship most noble hands without any pretension of my own Rights or of any other Person I beg leaue to subscribe.

Your Lorships most humble servant to Command

Thomas Duppa

January 4th 1685[99]

Secretary

Having an Occasion of sending my Secretary to London I haue Commanded him to Wayte upon you with this which is to thank you for your kind and discreet Management

---

[95] 2nd Baron Booth of Delamer.

[96] 1685/6.

[97] 1685/6.

[98] Presumably the lord great chamberlain.

[99] 1685/6.

[p. 58]

of my Affairs in my Absence I am very glad my Lord Duke[100] do so much honor my Offices as to Officiate for me when the King came to the House of peers[101] And I have writ to his Grace to do me the same fauour at my Lord Delamers Tryall which I can scarce be if I would for the shortness of the time & distance of Places

Your most Affectionate frend

to serue you

Lindsey

To Sir Thomas Duppa his Majesties Gentleman Usher of ye Black Rod

Richard Sparrow Servant to his Majesties Groom Porter Craveth Allowance of the Right Honourable John Earl of Mulgrave Lord Chamberlain of his Majesties Household for his Attendance on the House of Peers by the space of 49 Days Called May 19 1685 and continued sitting in Parliament till July ye 2nd 1685 and Adjourned till the 4th of August 1685 Then adjourned till the 9th of November 1685 Then continued sitting till ye 20th of the same Month Then Prorogued by the Commission till the 10th of February 1685[102] then Mett and Prorogued by

Com

[p. 59]

Commission till the 10th of May 1686 Then Mett and Prorogued by Commission til November 22th 1686 In all 49 days I now humbly Craue the usuall Allowance of 20d a day to be paid by the Treasurer of his Majesties Chamber

	l	s	d
This sum is £4	1	8

Wood and Coals against the Sitting of Parliament for the House of Peers the 19th of May 1685

It is desired by the Gentleman Usher of the Black Rod

1	That Six load of Tallwood	
2	Six loades of Billet	
3	12 hundred Weight of Scotch Coal	per Weeke
4	Twenty One Quarter of Charcoal	

to be sent to the Lords House for 12 Rooms there

Examined per Thomas Duppa Black Rod

Delivered for the House of Lords at Westminster this 22 November 1686

To the Woodyard Scullery per Diem

Charcoal	vij Quarters	
Tallwood	1½ load	
Billets	ij load	per John Sparrow
Scotch Coal	ccc	

---

[100] Presumably the 7th duke of Norfolk.

[101] At the prorogation on 20 Nov. 1685.

[102] 1685/6.

[p. 60]

Delivered for the House of Lords at Westminster this 14 November 1686

Charcoal	vij Quarters	
Talwood	1½ loads	
Billets	ij loads	} per Firebrace
Scottish Coal	3 c	

15 February 1686[103]

Pray deliver to my Servant Henry Griffiths for the use of the Lords House of Parliament this day & 12 White Wax lights and six Pounds of small Tallow lights
To the Officer Attending the Chandry   per Thomas Duppa Black Rod

Deliver for the House of Lords at Westminster ye 28 April 1687 at the Prorogation of the Parliament
To the Woodyard

Charcoal	3 quarters	
Talwood	1½	} per Firebrace
Billets	1 load	

Creditor

The Commissioners Names for the Proroguing of the Parliament from the 28 of April unto ye 22 November 1687

[p. 61]

Names of commissioners[104]

Die Lunae 22° Januarij[105] 1685
Order to black rod to take Gabriel Cox into custody; signed by John Browne, clerk of the parliaments

[p. 62]

Die Lunae 9° Julij 1660[106]

Upon hearing of Councill and Presidents this day at the Barr upon a Peticion of Humphrey Leigh[107] Serjeant at Armes Attending the Lord Chancellor Alexander Thayne[108] Gentleman Usher of the Black Rod Attending the House of Lords Defendants wherein the said Serjeant affirmed that all Warrants of that House ought to be directed to him for Apprehending and bringing of Delinquents before the Lords in Parliament and carrying them back into safe Custody The Lords entring into a Serious debate of the Matter and after due Consideration of the whole business. It is Ordered and declared by the Lords in Parliament assembled That their Lordships do reserve the power to themselves to Imploy what Persons they shall think fit

[103] 1686/7.

[104] Commissioners for prorogation. *LJ*, xiv, 97.

[105] *Sic.* An error for June. *LJ*, xiv, 53.

[106] *LJ*, xi, 85–6.

[107] Serjeant at arms 1660–73. *ORH*, i, 133.

[108] See p. 23 Note 9.

[p. 63]

for the sending Delinquents and keeping them in safe Custody as they shall see Cause

John Browne Clericus Parliamentorum[109]

December 1st 1688

Sir Thomas Duppas letter to the Lord Great Chamberlain[110]

May it please your Lordshipp

His Majesty having this day been pleased to Issue for his Proclamacion for the speedy calling a parliament I thought it my Duty to acquaint your Honour thereof and to send you the Proclamacion inclosed and to intreate your Lordship to send me the usual Letter from your Honor to my Lord Chamberlain of the Household to issue forth such Warrants to all Officers concerned under him, to make such Provisions for the Apparelling and making ready the House of Peers at Westminster as hath formerly been accustomed which I shall diligently take Care to be duely effected. And this with my humble services presented is the present business of

My honoured Lord

Your Lordshipps most Obedient Servant

Thomas Duppa Black Rod

To the Right Honourable ye Lord Chamberlain of England[111] at his house at Grimsthorpe[112] in Lincolnshire or at the Posthouse at Sanford[113]

[p. 64]

Sir

My Lord hath Commanded me to inclose this Letter Directed to my Lord Chamberlain to you,

And also a Copy of the same that you might see what his Lordship hath wrote. His Lordship doth not in the least doubt your Care in seeing the House of Peers fitted according to Lord Chamberlains directions against the time of their sitting. I have no more in Command but am

Your very humble servant

Robert Long[114]

To Sir Thomas Duppa Gentleman Usher of the Black Rod at Whitehall

December 3 1688

[109] MS gives 'Jo Browne Cleric Parliamento' rather than as elsewhere: 'Jo: Browne Cler (or Cleric:) Parl'.

[110] Written in another hand.

[111] An alternative designation for the lord great chamberlain.

[112] The principal seat of the earl of Lindsey.

[113] Presumably Stamford, 11 miles from Grimsthorpe.

[114] Probably the lord great chamberlain's secretary.

My Lord

Having received the Kings Proclamacion for calling a Parliament on the 25th January next, I desire your Lorship will Issue out your Warrant to those Officers therein concerned for the Apparelling and Accommodating the house of Peers Princes Lodgings and Painted Chamber with those necessaryes and conveniences as formerly hath been used upon

[p. 65]

the like occasion. I am

My Lord

Your Lordshepps most humble servant

Lindsey

A Copy of a letter to ye Lord Great Chamberlain of the Household

An Estimate of the Charges of Severall Necessaries for furnishing the House of Peers

Great Wardrobe   July 16th 1688

		li.	s.	d.
12	Tod of Wool used about the Packs Seets & Benches in the house of Peers	} 18:	00:	00
160	Ells of Canvas for Covering the Packs Seats and Benches	} 12:	00:	00
12	Pieces of large Crimson Say for covering the seates Benches Formes and Packs	} 68:	00:	00
	Making 4 great Sacks of Canvas & stuffing and covering them and all the seats Benches & Formes with Canvas and Say and all other Upholsterers Work and Materiall by him provided for the same	} 19:	16:	8
9	Large Pewter Candelsticks	2:	5:	00
4	Pair of other large Candelsticks	1:	00:	00
4	Pair of lesser Pewter Candelsticks	1:	4:	00
9	Pair of Snuffers	0:	9:	00
9	Necessary Stooles with two Pans to each Boat	8:	00:	00
9	Pewter Chamber potts about	2:	00:	00

[p. 66]

		li.	s.	d.
7	Dozen of Turky Work Chairs about	50:	00:	00
2	Yards of Green Cloth for a Carpet and 35 yards of Green Bayes to hang a Passage in the House of Peers	} 6:	00:	00
4	Pair of Andirions 4 pair of Creepers fireshovels and Tongs great firefolks 6 pair of Bellows and a perfuming Pan	} 13:	15:	00

£202: 15: 00

Goods to furnished the house of Peers

By the Groom Porter

6	Spanish Tables Oak	4:	00:	0
12	Double Benches for the Lordshouse	20:	00:	0
6	Single Sconces for ye Princes Room	8:	00:	0
6	Single Sconces for the Painted Chamber	6:	00:	0
6	Wall Plates	0:	15:	0
6	Half Lanthorns	0:	18:	0
2	Hole lanthorns	0:	8:	00
6	Pair of Bellowes	0:	12:	0
6	Pair of Snuffers	0:	15:	0
6	Pair of Andirons	9:	00:	0
6	Fireshovells & 6 Pair of Tongs	2:	00:	0

[p. 67]

	li	s	d
For furniture of three Chimneyes that is to say the Painted Chamber the Lords House and the Princes Chamber }		15: 00: 00	

In all £67: 18: 00

An estimate of Wood & Coales for the House of Peers

6	Load of Tallwood	3:	00:	00
6	Load of Billetts	3:	00:	00
12	Of Scotch Coal	0:	18:	00
21	Quarters of Charcoal	4:	14:	00
	Carryage	0:	18:	00
		12:	10:	00

Chandry

Torches 2 D[ozen]

Sizes for Tobacco 6lbweight

Wax lights 6 Dozen

Tallow lights 12 Dozen with per Week

> Or whats need full by Note from the Black Rod with a Chest to keep them in

Wood and Coales necessary to be sent to the house of Peers against the Meeting of the Convention the 22 day of January 1688/9

[p. 68]

For 12 Chimnyes

Winter Allowance

Talwood	1 load	
Billets	2 load	} per Diem
Scotch Coal	3 C	
Charcoal	7 Quarters	

The aboue being the allowance when there was but 9 Chimnies Now there are 12 Chymnies

These are to desire you to Attend with Black Rod of your Office at Westminster by 8 of the Clock to morrow morning being Wednesday the 13 instant And have your Horse ready to Assist Garter King of Arms at the Proclayming of King William & Queen Mary pursuant to the Declaration of the Lords Spiritual and Temporal and the Commons Assembled at Westminster and hereof fail not. Dated the 12th day of February 1688/9

Norfolk & Marshal

To Sir Thomas Duppa Knight Gentleman Usher of the Black Rod

[p. 69]

Die Jovis 28° Februarij 1688[115]

Order to Sir Thomas Duppa, black rod, for discharge of Benjamin Baker; signed by John Browne, clerk of the parliaments

Die Jovis 28 Februarij 1688[116]

Order to Sir Thomas Duppa, black rod, to secure Robert Clarke; signed by John Browne, clerk of the parliaments

[p. 70]

Die Jovis 28 Februarij 1688[117]

Order to Sir Thomas Duppa, black rod, to bring James Lepost[118] to the bar; signed by John Browne, clerk of the parliaments

Die Sabati 2° Martij 1688[119]

Order for Edward Aesley, a priest, now in custody of black rod to be brought before the lords of the council with his trunks; signed by John Browne, clerk of the parliaments

[p. 71]

Die Martij 5° 1688[120]

Order to Sir Thomas Duppa, black rod, for the discharge of Edward Aesley; signed by John Browne, clerk of the parliaments

April 22th 1689

The Parliament sate in January and February last 33 Dayes

That is in January	66 Quarters	
And in March last	26 Quarters	
There is due	52	
In all	<u>118 Quarters</u>	

Sir Thomas Duppa hath had of me at Whitehall }   6 Quarters

---

[115] 1688/9. *LJ*, xiv, 134.

[116] 1688/9. *LJ*, xiv, 134.

[117] 1688/9. *LJ*, xiv, 134.

[118] *LJ*, xiv, 134 gives 'Le Port'.

[119] 1688/9. *LJ*, xiv, 137.

[120] 1688/9. *LJ*, xiv, 139.

Now remaines		**112 Quarters**
In money		£16: 16: 20

[p. 72]

Sir Thomas Duppa Black Rod Prays Allowance for his Extraordinary Disbursements following By Order of the House of Peers since the 22th January 1688

For preparing and making ready the Lords House & Ayring ye Roomes	} 2: 00: 00
For Furnishing and providing 6 Dozen of Turky Work Chaires in the Prince's Lodgings and 7 other Roomes about the House	} 24: 00: 00
For 16 Large Pewter Candlesticks & 9 pair of Snuffers for several Roomes	} 4: 18: 00
For necessary Stoolds and double Pans and 9 Chamber Potts for the Lord's use	} 10: 00: 00
For a green Cloth Carpet & 35 yards of Green Say's to hang the Lobbys	} 6: 6: 00
For 4 pair of Andirons 4 pair of Creepers fireshovel Tongs 2 great Fireforks Bellow's & Perfuming Pans	} 13: 15: 00
To severall Messengers sent with Letters to the Lords Absent to appear & Attend the House by the Lords Order in several Counties Amounts to	} 25: 00: 0
	£85: 19: 00

[p. 73]

These Services have been performed and furnished by the Black Rod unto the last of February 1688/9

Lindsey Great Chamberlain

These are to signify unto your Lordshipp his Maiestys Pleasure That you Provide and Deliver unto Sir Thomas Duppa Knight Gentleman Usher Dayly Wayter to his Majesty and Gentleman Usher Black Rod A Robe of some Stuff and Fashion as was formerly delivered to the Gentleman Usher of the Black Rod against any Coronacion. And this shall be your Warrant. Given under my hand this 23th day of March 1668/9[121] in the first year of their Majesties Reign.

Dorsett[122]

To the Right Honorable the Lord Montagu Master of his Majestys Great Wardrobe and to his Deputy there

These are to require you to Cause to be Erected in the Painted Chamber a Court for the Lords Commissioners of the Claymes for his Maiestys Coronacion to ready

---

[121] An error for 1688/9.
[122] 6th earl of Dorset.

the 28th of this instant March. Given under my hand this 19th day of March In the first year

[p. 74]

of their Majesties King William & Queen Mary's Reign Annorum Domini 1688/9

Lindsey Great Chamberlain

To Francis Negus Esquire Secretary to the Right Honourable The Duke of Norfolk Earl Marshall

Die Sabati 27° Aprilis 1689[123]

Order to Sir Thomas Duppa, black rod, for the attendance of Sir Richard Holloway[124] and Sir Francis Withens;[125] signed by John Browne, clerk of the parliaments

[p. 75]

Die Veneris 3° May 1689[126]

Order for the attendance of Sir Richard Holloway and Sir Francis Withins; signed by John Browne, clerk of the parliaments

William Almont carried this Order and shewed it to Sir Francis Withins who read the same ye 3d May 1689

The house not sitting tomorrow has ordered you to Appear on Munday

Die Sabati 25° May 1689[127]

Order to Sir Thomas Duppa, black rod, to convey Titus Oates to the prison of king's bench; signed by John Browne, clerk of the parliaments

[p. 76]

May 25th 1689

I John Hancock,[128] Deputy to Sir Thomas Duppa did Convey the Body of Titus Oates into the Custody of Mr Philpott Marshall of Kings Bench this present Saturday being the 25th day of May 1689 In Witness whereof I haue herewith sett my hand this day and year aboue

John Hancox

May 28th 1689

Received then of Sir Thomas Duppa four letters of Summons vizt For the Duke of Newcastle[129] Earl of Exeter[130] Earl of Yarmouth[131] & Lord Coventry[132] to

---

[123] *LJ*, xiv, 194.

[124] Former justice of the king's bench. *ODNB*.

[125] Former justice of the king's bench. *ODNB*.

[126] *LJ*, xiv, 201.

[127] *LJ*, xiv, 221.

[128] Doorkeeper of the house of lords 1690–2. *CTB*, ix, 780, 1732.

[129] 2nd duke of Newcastle.

[130] 5th earl of Exeter.

[131] 2nd earl of Yarmouth.

[132] 5th Baron Coventry of Aylesborough.

appear at the house of Peers the sixth day of June and this Service I promise to perform and give Notice accordingly. Witness my hand the day above written

John Allen

Received then of Sir Thomas Duppa two letters from the House of Peers to summon

Lord Clarendon[133] and

[p. 77]

Lord Carlisle[134] which I promise to perform Witness my hand the day above written.

St John Tayler[135]

Die Mercurij 12 Junij 1689[136]

Order to Sir Thomas Duppa, black rod, to bring Serjeant Ingleby[137] to the bar; signed by John Browne, clerk of the parliaments

Die Lune 17° Junij 1689

Ordered by the Lords Committee[138] Appointed to draw up an Address touching the Isles of Wight Jersey Guernsey and Scilly &c That the Gentleman Usher of the Black Rod doe desire his Grace the Duke of Scombergh the Lord Viscount Hatton[139] the Lord Germin[140] Sir Henry Goodrick[141] Sir Henry Sheer[142] The Secretary of the Army and some

[p. 78]

of the Commissioners of the Admiralty to be in the Prince's Lodgings neer the house of Peers to Morrow at Nine of the Clock in the morning at which time their Lordships will further consider touching the said Address.

John Browne Clericus Parliamentorum

Die Lune 1 Julij 1689[143]

Order to Sir Thomas Duppa, black rod, to bring Richard Carter to the bar; signed by John Browne, clerk of the parliaments

[p. 79]

Die Martis 28° May 1689[144]

---

[133] 2nd earl of Clarendon.
[134] 2nd earl of Carlisle.
[135] A king's messenger; see below, p. 55.
[136] *LJ*, xiv, 241.
[137] Sir Charles Ingleby was a former baron of the exchequer. *ODNB*.
[138] For this committee see *LJ*, xiv, 244.
[139] 1st Viscount Hatton of Gretton.
[140] 2nd Baron Jermyn of St Edmundsbury.
[141] Sir Henry Goodricke. *HPC, 1660–1690*, iii, 410–12.
[142] Sir Henry Sheeres. *ODNB*.
[143] *LJ*, xiv, 262.
[144] *LJ*, xiv, 224–5.

Order to Sir Thomas Duppa, black rod, to bring Edward, Lord Griffin,[145] *in safe custody; signed by John Browne, clerk of the parliaments*

> A Copy of Sir Thomas Duppa's Privy Seal for 200li per Annum per King William

William and Mary by the Grace of God King and Queen of England Scotland France and Ireland Defender of the faith & To the Commissioners of our Treasury now being And the Treasurer and Under Treasurer

[p. 80]

of our Exchequer or Commissioners of our Treasury for the time being Greeting Whereas our trusty and well beloved Sir Thomas Duppa Knight Gentleman Usher Black Rod hath of late years by Virtue of severall Letters Patents been allowed and paid at the Receipt of the Exchequer the yearly Pension or sum of Two hundred Pounds in lieu of certain perquisites and all allowances by him released to the Crown And whereas it appears by the Certificate of our Right Councellour Sir Robert Howard Knight Auditor of the said Receipt of the Exchequer that the said Pension or sum of Two hundred pounds per Annum hath been paid to Michaelmas 1688 and no further Our Will and Pleasure is and we does hereby Authorise and Command that out of treasure now or hereafter being and remaining in ye Receipt of our Exchequer not appropriated to particular uses By Act of Parliament you pay or Cause to be paid to

him

[p. 81]

him the said Sir Thomas Duppa our Gentleman Usher Black Rod or to his Assigns the Sum of One Hundred and Fifty Pounds forthwith after passing of our Letters of Privy Seale for the three Quarters on the said Pension or yearly sum ended at the Nativity of St John Baptist now last past And the likely yearly sum of Two hundred Pounds from the Feast of St John Baptist last past quarterly at the four most usual Feasts or Termes in the yere by equall porcions during our Pleasure The same to goe and be inlieu of the said Perquisites and Allowances for which the same was formerly granted And these our Letters shall be your sufficient Warrant and Discharge in this behalf Given under our Privy Seale at our Pallace at Westminster the 25th July in the first year of our reign 1689

Thomas Watkins[146]

Die Lunae 12 Augusti 1689[147]

---

[145] 1st Baron Griffin of Braybrooke.

[146] Clerk of the privy seal, admitted 11 June 1672. TNA, PSO 5/11.

[147] *LJ*, xiv, 309.

Upon reading the peticion of Sir Thomas Duppa Gentleman Usher of the Black Rod and other Officers belonging to the House of Peers shewing That they find upon the Roll of Fees ancien[148]

[p. 82]

anciently established by the House belonging to the Officers attending thereon, there is a Fee of Thirty Shillings due to the Gentleman Usher of the Black Rod and ten shillings to the Yeoman Usher from the Members of this House who sends his Proxy and other Fees of entry due to him and the other Officers Attending this House upon any Lords first Sitting in Parliament And praying to have the antient Roll of Fees reinforced & the severall Fees paid And also Praying their Lordships Directions therein. It is thereupon Ordered by the Lords Spiritual and Temporal in Parliament assembled That the said Fees of Thirty Shillings and Ten Shillings and the other Fees of Entrance and Ancient Roll of Fees be and are hereby confermed and reinforced to the End they may be paid by all the Members of this House

John Browne Clericus Parliamentorum

[p. 83]

Die Veneris 2° Augusti 1689[149]

Order to Sir Thomas Duppa, black rod, for discharge of Henry Hutchings; signed by John Browne, clerk of the parliaments

Allowed in the Creditor of the Parliament House for Wood and Candles for the Month of April May and June 1688

White

[p. 84]

April	lb	oz	May	lb	oz	June	lb	oz
White Wax –	47	1⅔	76	8		76	4	
Yellow Wax –	37	½		30	0		18	0
Tallow lights –	30 Dozen			48 Dozen			24 Dozen	
Charcoal –	130 quarters			100 quarters			84 quarters	
Logg Wood –	39 load			27 load			20 load	
Billets –	39 load			27 load			25 load	
Scotch Coal –	3 Tons 18 c			2 Tons ½ c			1 Ton 17½ c	

Charcoal at 5 Quarters per diem
Logwood – 1 load per diem
Billets – 1½ load per diem
Scotch Coal – 3 C per diem

---

[148] *Sic.*

[149] *LJ*, xiv, 302.

Die Sabbati 26 October 1689[150]

Order to Sir Thomas Duppa, to bring Henry, earl of Peterborough, to the bar; signed by John Browne, clerk of the parliaments

[p. 85]

Die Martii 12° November 1689[151]

Order to Sir Thomas Duppa, black rod, to carry Richard, Viscount Preston, to the Tower; signed by John Browne, clerk of the parliaments

Die Lunae 11° November 1689[152]

Order to Sir Thomas Duppa, black rod, to take Richard, Viscount Preston, into custody; signed by John Browne, clerk of the parliaments

[p. 86]

Die Veneris 22° Novembris 1689

Ordered by the Lords Committees[153] appointed to consider who were the Advisers & prosecutors of the Murders of the Lord Russell[154] Cotton Sidney[155] Sir Thomas Armstrong[156] Mr Cornish[157] & Thomas Cornish Dr Chamberlain[158] Mr Attwood[159] & Mr Keeling[160] doe Attend the House of Peers on Munday next at Ten of the Clock in the forenoon to be sworn at the Barr in Order to their giving Informacion to the said Lords Committee at fiue of the Clock in the afternoon in the Princes Lodging neer the House of Peers And it is further Ordered That Sir Dudley North[161] doe attend the Lords Committee at the time and place aboue mentioned.

Jo Browne Clericus Parliamentorm

Die Martij 10° Decembris 1689[162]

Ordered that Anthony Vernatti do stand committed to black rod; signed by John Browne, clerk of the parliaments

---

[150] *LJ*, xiv, 326.

[151] *LJ*, xiv, 338.

[152] *LJ*, xiv, 337.

[153] For this committee see *LJ*, xiv, 331.

[154] Lord William Russell. *HPC, 1660–1690*, iii, 365–8; *ODNB*.

[155] Presumably a clerical slip for Colonel (Algernon) Sidney. *ODNB*.

[156] See *HPC, 1660–1690*, i, 544–5.

[157] Henry Cornish. *ODNB*.

[158] Hugh Chamberlain. See *LJ*, xiv, 331, 352.

[159] Willam Attwood. *ODNB*. See *LJ*, xiv, 331, 352.

[160] Josiah Kelyng. *ODNB*. See *LJ*, xiv, 354. Keeling did not make an appearance on 25 Nov. as instructed (*LJ*, xiv, 331) but was ordered to attend on the 27th (*LJ*, xiv, 331). He complied on 2 Dec. when two witnesses deposed against him and he was denied bail (*LJ*, xiv, 357–8). On 20 Dec. the contents of his examinations taken earlier were presented to the house (*LJ*, xiv, 377, 384–5, 387–8).

[161] See *HPC, 1660–1690*, iii, 149–51; *ODNB*.

[162] *LJ*, xiv, 367.

[p. 87]

Die Jovis 5 December 1689[163]

Upon reading the Peticion of Sir Roger Harsnett Knight Eldest Serjeant at Armes to the King and Queenes most excellent Majesties Praying (as he having the Honour to Attend the Speaker of this House as Serjeant at Arms) soe he may haue the Liberty to Execute the Orders of this House for taking into Custody such Persons as the House shall Order to be taken as his Predecessors have done and to receive such Fees for soe doing as haue been hereto fore accustomed. It is ordered by the Lords Spiritual and Temporal in Parliament Assembled That it be and is hereby referred to the Committee for Privileges to consider of the said Peticion and hear all Persons concerned therein, and make report to the House

John Browne Clericus Parliamentorum

7[164]

[p. 88]

7° Decembris 1689

To the Right Honourable the Lords of ye Committee for Priviledges in Parliament

The humble Peticion of Sir Thomas Duppa Black Rod

Sheweth   That your Peticioner was Constituted Gentleman Usher of the Black Rod at a Chapter held at Windsor the Sixth day of May 1683 as appears by Pattent under the Great Seal of the most Noble Order of the Garter.

That in the time of all Parliaments before and since It was the undoubted Right of his Predecessors to have the Commitment and custody of all Prisoners and Delinquents Committed by the House of Peers.

That the Serjeant At Armes that Atended the Lord Hallifax[165] during the time that he was Speaker in the Lords House, had Allowed him Ten shillings per diem for his Attendance and so to continue during the sitting of the Parliament which is a Certain Allowance to him.

And your Peticioners Fees are casual and uncertain.

He therefore humbly Prayes

[p. 89]

that your Lordships will be pleased to Inspect the antient Books of Orders & Rolls of Fees due to him in this Case and to Preserve your Peticion in the accustomed Rights and Dues of his Place.

And as in Duty bound he shall Pray &c

---

[163] *LJ*, xiv, 361.

[164] *Sic.*

[165] Speaker of the house of lords 22 Jan.–20 Sept. 1689.

The Case of Sir Thomas Duppa Black Rod in Answer to Serjeant Harsnett's Peticion to take away his Fees to be heard the 17th of December 1689

Written by Mr Reading

The Black Rod by his Pattent is to Attend the House of Lords and their Lordships considering his constant Attendance on them within their Doores whilst they sitt and in their respective Roomes and Lobbyes and at their Committees both early and late Have often been pleased to Confirme and reinforce the Antient Roll of Fees and particularly that for Executing their Commitment Orders.

The Serjeant is no wayes Capable of doing any part of this Duty and hath Ten shillings a day allowed him aboue all

[p. 90]

the other Fees of his Mace for Wayting on the Speaker only without Doores.

If any of his Predecessors Executed any of their Lordships Orders for Commitments It either was with the Consent of, Or to the Prejudice of the Black Rod

The Black Rod enjoyes not the Serjeant's new Fee[166] and he humbly hopes their Lordships who dayly see his diligent and Dutifull Observance of them will not permitt one who doth their Lordships no shadow of Service to carry away the Chiefest of his Perquisites.

The Black Rod's Case in Answer to the Peticion of the Serjeant at Arm's now Attending the Speaker in the house of Peers

1. That the present Serjeant is no Officer of the Lords house
2. That he hath the Allowance of Ten shillings per Diem for his Attendance paid by Sir Robert Howard at the Exchequer and doth no other Service for any of the Lords. And is not the Serjeant of Attending the Great Seale, who (if any) has a greater pretence to it
3. That by Pattent under the Great Seale

[p. 91]

of the most Honourable Order of the Garter The Black Rod is to hold the said office together with the Custody of the litle Park at Windsor and all other Priviledges, Fees perquisites Immunities, Ensigns Rights and Liberties whatsoever belonging thereunto in as full and ample manner as Sir Edward Carteret or any other possessing the said Office did or ought to have enjoyed the same & which he humbly Prayes may be read and the Serjeant and Pattent also and then considered by your Lordships.

4. That at the joyfull time of King Charles the Second's Restauracion when the Lord Chancellor Hyde was the Great Minister of State Serjeant Leigh then attending the Great Seale &c might obteyne fauour of the Lords to take some Delinquents and bring them to the Black Rod by Agreement with Sir John Aiton who then newly entered into that office &c

---

[166] Presumably the 10*s*. per diem referred to above.

All which and the many other Dayly Services of the Black Rod is humbly submitted to your Lordships considerations

The Prince of Orange's Warrant to Sir Thomas Duppa &c

Wee doe hereby require you to giue Order to the Removing Wardrobe to furnish

[p. 92]

both Houses of Parliament and the Rooms thereunto belonging as heretofore has been accustomed to be done and that you give order to Mr Surveyor of the Works to mend the Matting and Glass the Windows and what is necessary to be done by his Office And also that you give Orders to the officers of the Board of Greencloth to give such allowances of Wood for fire in the House of Lords as was heretofore allowed and that you cause both Houses & Rooms adjoining to be made ready with all things necessary as usually it was done at the Meeting of Parliament And this shall be your Warrant. Given at St James's this 18th day of January 1688.[167]

Prince D'Orange

To Sir Thomas Duppa Knight Gentleman Usher and Black Rod

Whereas his Majesty hath thought fitt that the Furniture in the House of Lords shall continue as it is during this Sessions Only with the Alterations following (vizt) These are therefore to signify unto your Lordships his Majesties Pleasure That you cause the two Frames of the two Stooles on both sides

[p. 93]

the Cloth of State in the house of Lords to be covered with Crimson Velvet on both sides and Gold and Silver Lace as formerly accustomed And this shall be your Lordships Warrant. Given under my hand this 26th day of April 1690 In the Second year of their majesties Reign

Dorsett

To the Right honourable the Earl of Montague Master of his Majesties Great Wardrobe and his Deputy there

Die Veneris 25 Aprilis 1690[168]

Order for discharge of William Hempson; signed by John Browne, clerk of the parliaments

Die Veneris 25° Aprilis 1690[169]

Order to black rod to bring John Washington to the bar; signed by John Browne, clerk of the parliaments

---

[167] 1688/9.

[168] *LJ*, xiv, 474.

[169] *LJ*, xiv, 474.

[p. 94]

I doe hereby Authorize & Appoint St John Taylor, one of his Majesties Messengers, or William Clayton or either of them my Deputy for the Execucion of this Order

Thomas Duppa Black Rod

A Copy

[p. 95]

A Copy of the Names of the Peers that were Authorized by their Majesties Commission to Prorogue the Parliament from the 7th of July to the 28th of the same month[170]

All to be in their Robes

Names

The Black Rods Message to the Commons 1690

Mr Speaker

The Lords Authorised by Virtue of their Majesties Commission Desire the

[p. 96]

Attendance of this Honourable House in the House of Peers to hear the said Commission read.

The Commons being brought up (By the Black Rod) to the Barr of the House of Lords The Commission being read The Lord President[171] sitting on a Bench placed aboue the Woolpack with the seal in Commission Signified That it was their Majesties Pleasure the Parliament should be Prorogued from the 7th to the 28th of July 1690 And the Parliament was prorogued to the 28th July.

The Parliament Mett the 28th of July 1690 And by Virtue of their Majesties Commission was Prorogued to the 18th of August following By the Lord President in the forme and manner aboue written All the Lords of the Council being in the said Commission as in the other of the 7th of July.

The Parliament Mett the 18th of August 1690 and was Prorogued by Commission in manner and forme as in the 7th of July &c to the 8th September following.

Note that the Commons adjourned from Munday the 8th of September to Thursday the 11th

The Parl

[p. 97]

The Parliament mett the 8th of September 1690 and the Lords adjourned themselves to Friday following being the 12th of September at her Majesties request by the Lord President.

---

[170] For this and the following prorogations and adjournments see *LJ*, xiv, 505–15, 618–19; *CJ*, x, 424–6.
[171] Marquess of Carmarthen.

The Parliament Mett on Friday the 12th of September and by his Majesties Commission was Prorogued to the 2d of October following &c.

The Parliament Mett on Thursday the 2d of October which day the King came to the House of Peers and made a Speech all the Lords being in their robes And the Commons brought up by Black Rod to the Barr of the House Then the House adjourned to Munday following.

Note that a Session began this 2d of October 1690 and sat till the 5th of January following when they adjourned to the last of March next ensuing

The House mett on Munday the 6th of October and proceeded to buisiness viz ut sequitur[172]

Die Jovis 9° Octobris 1690[173]

Order to Sir Thomas Duppa, black rod, to bring John Bernard and Jacob Broad to the bar: signed by John Browne, clerk of the parliaments

[p. 98]

20th February 1689[174]

May it Please your Lordship[175]

Upon a Serious Survey of ye furniture of the Lords House the Princes Lodging and all the other Rooms and Lobbys belonging therunto I find the Woolsacks and Benches very bare and worn out

[p. 99]

to the Canvas and all the Matting in & about the House of Lords worn and torn to pieces And there being a New Velvet State Cushion stooles and Chairs about the Throne Ordered to be ready for the opening of the New Parliament the 20th of March next I humbly leave it to your Lordships Consideration whether you will be pleased to acquaint the Lord Chamberlain of the Household[176] therewith by Letter and advise that the fault may not lye at your Lordships or my Neglect. Besides at the Dissolution of every Parliament the Custome ever was, That the old furniture was the Black Rods Fees By Antient Customs, except the Kings Hangings & State &c which are returned to the removing Wardrobe for his Majesties further use All which is herewith humbly offered to your Lordships Judgment By

My Lord

Your Obedient humble Servant

Thomas Duppa Black Rod

The 7th November 1690

Be it remembered that the day & year above said Mr John Whinwood[177] Dyed

---

[172] So be it.

[173] *LJ*, xiv, 519–20.

[174] 1689/90.

[175] The lord great chamberlain.

[176] The earl of Dorset.

[177] An error for 'Whinyard'.

[p. 100]

and was Buryed at St Margaret's Westminster the 13th of November And upon the 15th of the same at the request of Sir Thomas Duppa Gentleman Usher of the Black Rod In Consideracion of a Sum of Monyes then Paid him by Mr Benjamin Cooling[178] to the said Sir Thomas Duppa Who upon the 15th of the said Month Prevailed with the Right Honourable the Earl of Rochester who Acquainted the House of Lords then Sitting That the said Mr Whinyard being dead and buryed It was the Right of the Black Rod to putt in a Yeoman Usher under him into the said Place which in due respect to their Lordships he desired they might be acquainted with.

Whereupon the Earl of Macklesfield made some Question whether the Lord Great Chamberlain had no Claim to it Upon which the Black Rods Pattent was called for and ready by the Clerk at the Table which gave the Lords full satisfaction. And the Lords Hallifax and Rochester declared then that their Lordships had nothing to doe in it.

Thereupon the Black Rod called

[p. 101]

the said Mr Benjamin Cooling into the House and putt him into Wayting in the said Place of Yeoman Usher.[179]

Note a Sessions began this 22nd October 1690[180]

The Parliament Mett the 22th of October And the King came to the House of Peers and made a Speech And then the House proceeded to buisiness.

Die Mercurij 18 November 1691[181]

Order for the attendance of Sir Ralph Delaval and others; signed by Matthew Johnson,[182] clerk of the parliaments

The Black Rods deputacion for the executing this Order as followeth

I do hereby Authorize & Appoint George Cooling one of the Kings Messengers as my Deputy for the serving this Order

18 November 1691   Thomas Duppa Black Rod

[p. 102]

A Copy of George Coolings Bill for Executing the Order abouesaid

	li	s	d
Sent with an Order of the House of Lords to Portsmouth to Sir Ralph Delaval Captain Martin Captain Gillam Mr Battin and a French Captain to Summon them to Appear before the House	3.	8.	0
it being to Portsmouth and back again 136 Miles at 6d per Mile For 13 Stages at 2d per Stage	1.	6.	0

---

[178] Son of William Cooling of Shropshire. Assistant secretary to the lord chamberlain 1660–97; keeper of the council chamber 1675–1700; yeoman usher 1690–1700. Died 2 Dec. 1700. E. Hatton, *New View of London* (2 vols, 1708), i, 341.

[179] See *Manuscripts of the House of Lords*, new ser., iv, 146.

[180] An error for 1691. *LJ*, xiv, 625.

[181] *LJ*, xiv, 652.

[182] See Appendix: Biographical Notes.

For hire of a Boat to goe aboard the Fleet   0. 10. 0

Being in this Service 3 dayes at the usual rate of 10s per Diem   110. 0

£6. 14. 0

Die Mercurij 18 Novembrij 1691

Entred supra

1° Die Decembris 1691[183]

Order for the attendance of Captain Beaumont and Captain Munden

[p. 103]

Die Veneris 7 Novembris 1691[184]

Lady Francis Holford to attend the House

Order for the attendance of Lady Frances Holford/Halford; signed by John Browne, clerk of the parliaments

Die Veneris 7° Novembris 1691[185]

Order to Sir Thomas Duppa, black rod, to bring Lady Frances Holford/Halford to the bar; signed by John Browne, clerk of the parliaments

[p. 104]

Die Sabati 8° Novembris 1691[186]

Order to black rod to bring Lady Frances Holford/Halford to the bar to answer for her contempt; signed by John Browne, clerk of the parliaments

Die Lunae 4 Januarij 1691[187]

Order to Sir Thomas Duppa, black rod, to convey Lord Morley and Mounteagle[188] to the Tower of London; signed by Matthew Johnson, clerk of the parliaments

Tower January ye 4th 1691/2

Received then of Sir Thomas Duppa Usher of the Black Rod the Right Honourable

[p. 105]

the Lord Morley

Lucas[189]

Die Mercurij 16° Decembris 1691[190]

Order for the attendance of Sir Charles Hero; signed by Matthew Johnson, clerk of the parliaments

Die Mercurij 16 December 1691[191]

[183] *LJ*, xiv, 668.

[184] An error for 1690. *LJ*, xiv, 543.

[185] An error for 1690. *LJ*, xiv, 543–4.

[186] *LJ*, xiv, 544.

[187] *LJ*, xv, 15–16.

[188] 15th Lord Morley and Monteagle.

[189] 3rd Baron Lucas, governor and commander in chief of the Tower of London.

[190] *LJ*, xiv, 689.

[191] *LJ*, xiv, 689.

Order to Sir Thomas Duppa, black rod, to bring Lieutenant Primrose and the Serjeant at the Playhouse to the bar; signed by Matthew Johnson, clerk of the parliaments

George

[p. 106]

George Wilsons Fees Ordered by the House of Peers for the Lord Morley to Pay

	li	s	d
To the Black Rod for his Attachment Fee	3.	6.	8.
For the Riding 400 Miles	20:	0:	0.
For 22 days in Custody	22.	0:	0.
For his Discharge to ye Black Rod	3.	6.	8.
To the Clerk of the Parliament for his Discharge	3.	6.	8.
To the Yeoman Usher	1.	0.	0.
To the Clerk Assistant	1.	0.	0.
For the Orders of Attachment & Discharge	3.	6.	8.
For reading his Peticion	0.	2.	0.
This Sum to Thomas Shirley[192]	£55:	11:	0
The Lord Morley's Fees			
To the Black Rod for Attachment Fees	6:	6:	8
For his Carrying to the Tower	6:	6:	8
For his Discharge to the Black Rod	3:	6:	8
	£16:	0:	0
To Clerk of Parliament	3.	6.	8
Clerk Assistant	1.	0.	0
Yeoman Usher	1.	0.	0
2 Orders	1.	9.	0
	6.	15.	8
sum total	£78.	6.	8

[p. 107]

	li.	s.	d.
Mr George Wilson's Fees to ye Clerk and Yeoman Usher	6:	17:	8
Lord Morley's Fees to them	6:	17:	8
	13:	15:	8
Sir Thomas Duppa's Fees for both Attachments	22:	15:	4
To the Serjeant[193] & Mr Shirley	45:	0;	0

22th October 1692

May it Please your Lordship[194]

---

[192] Serjeant at arms 1692–d. Deputed by black rod to execute warrants 1690. Assigned to speaker of the house of lords 1692–3. Died 1701. *ORH*, i, 39–40, 167.

[193] Sir Roger Harsnett.

[194] The lord great chamberlain.

I hope this may find your Honour in good health and able to come up to Attend his Majesty and the House of Peers the 4th of November next at the Sitting of Parliament where I shall think my self happy in Obeying your Lordship's Commands.

In the mean time I think it my Duty to acquaint your Honour that the Old House of Commons will be ready for them to sitt in by the time appointed[195] And the Court of Requests having been built up & fitted for the house of Commons to Meet in during the Rebuilding of the Old House I conceive your Lordships Furniture which was erected in that Place.

I suppose as soon as the Old House is ready the New will be Ordered to be taken down by Sir Christopher Wren that built it. I humbly beg your Lordships Pardon

[p. 108]

for this Presumption And if I may be in any ways serviceable to your Honour herein be pleased to Command the Utmost Endeavours of

My Lord

your Lordships Obedient Servant

Thomas Duppa

To the Lord Great Chamberlain

Memorandum another Letter to the Lord Great Chamberlain in answer to his Lords That the Surveyor Obstructs the taking down the Boards and Furniture in the Court of Requests, because there was no use made of it by the House of Commons.

NB   Here was Mr Churchill[196] the stationers Two Bills[197]

To all to whom these Presents shall come, Greeting, Know yee That Sir Thomas Duppa, Gentleman Usher of the Black Rod to their present Majesties have Deputed & Appointed and by these presents do Depute & Appointed Sir Roger Harsnett knight and Thomas Shirley, Gentleman joyntly and severally. First for the Executing all Warrants and Orders for the Attaching of any Delinquents according to and in pursuance of the Lords House in

[p. 109]

Parliament (Peers excepted). Secondly That in Consideration thereof the said Sir Roger Harsnett and Thomas Shirley shall be answerable and Pay to the said Sir

---

[195] During repair work on the house of commons in 1692, contingency arrangements were made for MPs to meet in the court of requests when parliament reassembled. *HKW*, v, 401–3. The work advanced so speedily that they had no need of these arrangements (see below). The makeshift accommodation was taken down on 3 Nov. Narcissus Luttrell, *A Brief Historical Relation* (6 vols, Oxford, 1857), ii, 607.

[196] William Churchill (1661–1737), bookseller, bookbinder and stationer to the crown. *HPC, 1690–1715,* iii, 552–5; *HPC, 1715–1754,* i, 553.

[197] *Sic.* It looks as though copies of two of Churchill's bills appeared at this point in the master copy of the commonplace book.

Thomas Duppa or his Assigns for all such Orders as they so execute the sum of Thirty three shillings & 4d and half the daily Fees of Twenty shillings until the Delinquents be brought to the Bar of the Lords House and taken into Custody by the said Black Rod. And Thirdly and lastly That Sir Roger Harsnett and Thomas Shirley are to have all the Wills[198] money for themselves as their Due & Proper Fees. In Witness whereof Wee have here unto sett our Hands and Seals the first day of May in the [blank] year of the Reign of our Soveraign Lord and Lady William and Mary by the Grace of God King of England France and Ireland Defender of the Faith &c Annoque Domini 1690.

The Fore Session of Parliament begun the 4th

Articles of Agreement Intended had made and concluded by and between Sir Thomas Duppa Knight Gentleman Usher of the Black Rod Attending the

[p. 110]

most Honourable house of Lords and Thomas Shirley Esquire Serjeant at Armes Attending the Speaker of the said most Honourable House of Lords in manner and forme following First the said Sir Thomas Duppa do Covenant and agree to and with the said Thomas Shirley That he will from henceforth Depute and Appoint and he doth by these present Depute and Appoint the said Thomas Shirley for the Executing all Warrants and Orders for the Attaching of any Delinquents according to and in pursuance of the Lords House in Parliament (Peers Excepted) which said Warrants are to be directed to Sir Thomas Duppa and by Virtue of this Deputation executed by the said Thomas Shirley

Secondly. And the said Thomas Shirley doth Covenant and agree to and with the said Thomas Duppa That if he shall receive the Fees Commonly called the Day Fees of any such Person or Delinquent he shall Pay One Moyety thereof to the said Sir Thomas Duppa. And the said Sir Thomas Duppa doth Covenant to and with the said Thomas Shirley that if he shall receive the Fees commonly called the day Fees of any such Person or Delinquent he shall Pay One Moiety thereof to the said Thomas Shirley. It being

the[199]

[p. 111]

Intent of both Parties to these present that all the Fees growing due after the taking of the Delinquents or Persons soe Committed shall be equally divided between the said Sir Thomas Duppa and the said Thomas Shirley till the Person shall be taken into the Custody of the Black Rod. In Witness whereof both the parties aboue named haue to these present article sett their hands and Seals the second day of December in the 4th year of their Majesties reign King William and Queen Mary Annoque Domini 1692.

Thomas Duppa Black Rod

---

[198] *Sic.*

[199] *Sic.*

Thomas Shirley Serjeant at Arms

Die Martis 22 Novembris 1692[200]

It is Ordered by the Lords Spiritual and Temporal in Parliament Assembled that No Person shall be admitted to come into the House when the King is present Except such Strangers as the Lord Great Chamberlain shall think fitt And the Gentleman Usher & Yeoman Usher shall be punished if this Order be not strictly observed.

That no Peers son's be permitted whilst the House is sitting to come further into the House then the Footsteps of the Throne, Nor before the Archbishop's Bench.

That the Table in the House be sunck about six Inches lower and the Seat on which the Clerks sitt proportionably and a Place

[p. 112]

sunk in the Flooers for their feet.[201]

Die Sabati 7° die Decembris 1692[202]

Order to Sir Thomas Duppa, black rod, to bring Vincent Head, Richard Watts and Richard Hayes to the bar; signed by Matthew Johnson, clerk of the parliaments

Die Jovis 17° Novembris 1692[203]

[p. 113]

Order to Sir Thomas Duppa, black rod, to bring John Ballet to the bar; signed by Matthew Johnson, clerk of the parliaments

Die Mercurij 23° Novembris 1692[204]

It is ordered by the Lords Spiritual & Temporal in Parliament Assembled The Lords with the White Staves[205] and the Earl of Oxford, The Earl of Bridgwater[206] and the Earl of Macklesfield doe Attend his Majesty with the Address of this House in the behalf of the Lord Chief

[p. 114]

Baron Atkins[207] now Speaker of this House

Mathew John Clerk [of] Parliament

---

[200] *LJ*, xv, 122.

[201] The date for the creation of the pit enabling the clerk of the parliaments and his deputies to sit at a table to do their work rather than kneel at a woolsack is not known. But to judge from the provision being extended in Nov. 1692 it must have been sometime earlier. The purpose of the pit was not so much the comfort of the clerk and his staff as the convenience of the peers, enabling them to have an undisrupted view of the lord chancellor or whoever substituted for him in presiding over the assembly, and he of them.

[202] Incorrectly dated. It should read 17 Dec. 1692. A similar, but not identically, misdated entry appears for the same item on p. 64.

[203] *LJ*, xv, 113.

[204] *LJ*, xv, 123.

[205] The lord steward and lord chamberlain of the royal household.

[206] 3rd earl of Bridgwater.

[207] Sir Robert Atkyns (1620–1710), chief baron of the court of exchequer 1689–94; speaker of the house of lords 1689–93. *ODNB*; *HPC, 1660–1690*, i, 568–8.

Die Lunae 28° Novembris 1692[208]

Order to Sir Thomas Duppa, black rod, to bring Hugh Jones the elder, Hugh Jones the younger and Charles Skull to the bar; signed by Matthew Johnson, clerk of the parliaments

Die Mercurij 4° Januarij 1692[209]

Order to Sir Thomas Duppa, black rod, for the discharge of John Gregson; signed by Matthew Johnson, clerk of the parliaments

[p. 115]

Die Mercurij 18° Januarij 1692[210]

Order to Sir Thomas Duppa, black rod, for the discharge of John White; signed by Matthew Johnson, clerk of the parliaments

Die Veneris 20° Januarij 1692[211]

Order to Sir Thomas Duppa, black rod, for the attendance of Edmund Bohun and Richard Baldwin; signed by Matthew Johnson, clerk of the parliaments

[p. 116]

Die Lunae 17° Decembris 1692[212]

Order to Sir Thomas Duppa, black rod, to bring Vincent Head, Richard Watts and Richard Hayes to the bar; signed by Matthew Johnson, clerk of the parliaments

Die Sabati 31 Decembris 1692[213]

[p. 117]

Order to Sir Thomas Duppa, black rod, for the discharge of Richard Watts alias Waterman, Vincent Head and Richard Hayes; signed by Matthew Johnson, clerk of the parliaments

30th March 1675/6

Exp   Apud Westmonasterium Tricesimo die Marcij Regni Regis Caroli Secundi Tricesimo[214]

May it Please your Most Excellent Majesty

This conteines your Majesties Grant unto Elizabeth Whinyard Daughter of John Whinyard Esquire of the Office of Keeper of the Royall House within the Royall Palace of Westminster with the usual Fee of six pence by the day Payable out of the Exchequer To hold the said Offices to ye said Elizabeth and Ann[215] in Revercion after

---

[208] *LJ*, xv, 127.

[209] 1692/3. *LJ*, xv, 172.

[210] 1692/3. *LJ*, xv, 188.

[211] 1692/3. *LJ*, xv, 192.

[212] The day is incorrectly given. It should be Saturday (*Sabbati*), 17 Dec. 1692. A similarly, but not identically, misdated entry for the same item appears on p. 63.

[213] *LJ*, xv, 168.

[214] The following grant was embodied in letters patent under the great seal dated 8 May 1676. The keepership in question was commonly known as 'the housekeeper of the house of lords'. See Sainty, 'Office of Housekeeper', 56–60.

[215] Another daughter of John Whinyard. Sainty, 'Office of Housekeeper', 258.

[p. 118]

the death surrender or forfeiture of the said John Whinyard (who now enjoys the said office) successively with all other Priviledges and Advantage thereunto belonging during their respective lives.

A Fair Copy   Francis Winnington[216]

27° Marcij 1676

Signed William Rex King

Wee will and Command that immediately upon Sight hereof you deliver or cause to be delivered unto our Well beloved Servant Sir Thomas Duppa Knight Gentleman Usher of the Black Rod for Furnishing and making ready the Court Erected in Westminster Hall for the Tryall of Charles Lord Mohun[217] those parcells hereafter following That is to say Two and Twenty pieces of Say of the larger Size One hundred and Sixty Ells of Canvas to make Sacks and to Cover Stooles and Formes Twenty Tod of Wool for stuffing the Formes and Stooles within the Court And that you Pay for the Hay to fill the said Sacks And that you provide Threed, Layer and Nailes and Pay for the Workmanship

[p. 119]

of all the premises And that you furnish whatsoever eles shall be needfull for that Service That the Court may be after such manner as our Lord Great Chamberlain shall giue directions apparelled covered and furnished against this appointed Day And these our Letters signed with our owne hand shall be your sufficient Warrant Given under our Signet at our Palace of Westminster the 19thd day of January in the first year of our Reign.[218]

May it Please your most Excellent Majesty

This containes your Majesties Warrant to the Master of your Great Wardrobe for delivering of divers necessaries for furnishing the Court of Westminster Hall against the Tryall of Charles Lord Mohun And is done by order of the Right Honourable the Lord Chamberlain of their Majesties Honourable Household signifying your Majesties pleasure therein.

This is a true copy signed by His Majesty

January 31.

My Lord your Lordship will Please to Issue out your Warrant to the Great Wardrobe for furnishing the Court Erected in Westminster Hall for the Tryall of the Lord Mohun with Sockets Sconces and Candlesticks

With respect

Your Lordship's humble Servant

---

[216] Solicitor-general 1660–90. *ODNB; HPC, 1660–1690*, iii, 745–8; *HPC, 1690–1715*, v, 895–9.

[217] 4th Baron Mohun of Okehampton.

[218] An error for 'fourth year of our Reign'. The correct date is 19 Jan. 1692/3.

Lindsey Great Chamberlain

[p. 120]

These are to signify unto your Lordship his Majesties Pleasure That you deliver for the Service of the House of Peers Close stools with Boxes and Panns 6 Chamber potts 12 Pewter Candelstickes of the largest with Nozells to them and Snuffers and this shall be your Warrant Given under my hand this 28th of January 1692 in the fourth year of their Majesties Reign.[219]

Dorsett[220]

To the Right Honourable the Earl of Montague Master of the Great Wardrobe
The sessions began this 7th of November 1693[221]

His Majesty in his Royall Robes came the 7th November 1693 To His House of Peers and made a gracious Speech &c Then the House of peers adjourned to the 10th.

These are to signify unto your Lordship his Majesties Pleasure that you Provide and deliver unto Sir Thomas Duppa Knight Gentleman Usher Dayly Wayter and Black Rod These particulars following for the use of his Majesty in the House of Peers Twelve long Pewter Candelsticks the former being too short Twelve Pewter Chamber potts and Twelve pair of Snuffers And this shall be your Lordships Warrant Given under my hand

[p. 121]

this 10th of November 1693 in the fifth year of their Majesties Reign.

Dorsett

To the Right Honourable the Earl Montagu Master of their Majestys Great Wardrobe or to his Deputy there

Die Veneris 17° Novembris 1693[222]

Order to Sir Thomas Duppa, black rod, to bring Hugh Jones the elder and Hugh Jones the younger to the bar; signed by Matthew Johnson, clerk of the parliaments

Die Mercurij 22° Novembris 1693[223]

[p. 122]

Order to Sir Thomas Duppa, black rod, for the discharge of Joseph King and John Davis; signed by Matthew Johnson, clerk of the parliaments

Die Martij 2° Januarij 1693[224]

Order for Sir Thomas Duppa, black rod, for the discharge of John Carter and John Browne; signed by Matthew Johnson, clerk of the parliaments

---

[219] 1692/3.
[220] Lord chamberlain.
[221] *LJ*, xv, 19.
[222] *LJ*, xv, 300.
[223] *LJ*, xv, 19.
[224] 1693/4. *LJ*, xv, 331.

[p. 123]

Die Sabathi 18 November 1693[225]

Order to Sir Thomas Duppa, black rod, to bring John Davis and Joseph King to the bar; signed by Matthew Johnson, clerk of the parliaments

Die Veneris 15° Decembris 1693[226]

Ordered by the Lords Spiritual and Temporal

[p. 124]

in Parliament Assembled That John Rutter do Attend this house on Thursday the one and twentieth of this instant December at Ten of the Clock in the forenoooon

Mathew Johnson Clerk [of] Parliament

To Sir Thomas Duppa Gentleman Usher of the Black Rod &c & every of them

Die Sabati 10 Februarij 1693[227]

Order to Sir Thomas Duppa, black rod, to attach Thomas Price; signed by Matthew Johnson, clerk of the parliaments

Die Lunae 12° Februarij[228]

[p. 125]

Order to Sir Thomas Duppa, black rod, for the discharge of Thomas Price; signed by Matthew Johnson, clerk of the parliaments

Book Orders Anno 40[229] Page 110

Die Jovis 18 Februarij 1693[230]

Ordered &c That all Warrants for Apprehending of Delinquents and bringing them before this Honourable House are to be Directed to James Maxwell Esquire Gentleman Usher of the Black Rod Attending this House and he and none eles but such as he shall Appoint are to execute the same

Book Orders Anno 1640

> Page 24
> Page 124
> 154
> 171
> 193
> 199
> 305
> 316
> 355
> 488

All directed to the Black Rod for Attaching of Persons

---

[225] *LJ*, xv, 301.

[226] This order does not appear in *LJ*.

[227] 1693/4. *LJ*, xv, 365.

[228] 1693/4. *LJ*, xv, 366.

[229] This volume is in the Parliamentary Archives, HL/PO/JO/10/5/10.

[230] Corrected from 1633. Even so, an error for '1640' (1640/1) (*LJ*, iv, 166) where the word 'court' replaces the word 'House'.

[p. 126]

Pro William Churchill

The Stationers Bill to the House of Peers from July 1690 to December 1690

		li	s	d
July	One ream of Superfine Horn Cutt and folded One Ream of Superfine large Dutch Post 4o Gill and one Ream of Dutch large Post in 4o Cut and folded	3.	10.	0
	A Brasse Frame with a Wax Candle	1.	15.	0
	A Box of Wafers & 100 of Penns	0.	12.	0
October	7th Two Reams of superfine horn Cut and folded a fine Brasse Frame with Candls and 200 of the best Dutch Pens	4.	7.	0
	A leather Bottle with Inck and a pound of the best perfumed sealing Wax	0.	11.	0
9th	200 of the best Dutch Pens a Bag of White Sand and a leather Bottle with Inck	0.	17.	0
17th	Three ream of superfine horn Cutt and folded 3 Reames of superfine horn in 4to Cut and folded Two Brass Frames with Wax Candls 300 of Pens and 2 Razor Mettal Penknives	17.	13.	0
	2 Reames finest larg Post Dutch Post gilt in 4to and 2 Reames of the same Cut and folded	5.	0.	0
	3 Reames super fine horn Cut and folded two pounds best perfumed Sealing Wax 200 of the best Dutch Pens a large Brass Frame with wax Candls and a large Box Wafers	6.	8.	0
		£20.	13.	0

[p. 127]

		li	s	d
October 30	Two leather Bottles with Inck 3lb of the best perfumed	1.	15.	6
	Sealing Wax and a large Box of Wafers	1.	15.	6
	Two Reams of finest horn folio Cut and folded 2 Reams super fine large Dutch Post in 4to Cut and folded & one Ream of large Dutch post in 4tp Gilt	5.	10.	6
	A leather Bottle with inck and two hundred of the best Dutch pens	0.	15.	0
November 18	Two Reames superfine horn folio Cut and folded One Ream finest large Dutch Post in 4to Cut and folded And one Ream of finest Dutch large Post in 4to Gilt	4.	10.	0
	A fine Brass Frame with Candls and 2 Reams of superfine horn Cutt and folded	3.	15.	0
	A large Pocket Book in Green Vellum flapps and Clasps a Book 5 Quire fine Horn in Green Vellum Flap and One of the same of four Quire	1.	16.	0
		48.	4.	6

The Stationers Bill to the House of Peers

from May 1691 to January 1691

May	Two Reames super fine horn Cut and folded Two Reames of the finest Dutch Post in 4to Cut & folded A fine Brass frame with Wax Candls A large Box of Wafers and a hundred of the best Dutch Pens A leather Bottle with Inck a pound of the best perfumed Sealing Wax } 6. 17. 0

[p. 128]

		li. s. d
October 22th	Two Reames of Superfine horn Cutt & folded Two Reames of the finest large Dutch Post 4to Gilt Two Reames of the same Cutt & folded	} 7. 0. 0
	One Ream of the finest Horn in 4to Gilt	} 1. 0. 0
	Two Reams of the small Dutch Post 4to Cut and folded	} 1. 10. 0
	3 hundred of the best Dutch Pens a large Box of Wafers a pound of best perfumed Sealing Wax	} 1. 11. 6
	Two Reames of the finest Dutch Post large in 4to and 2 Reames of the finest horn folio Cut and folded	} 5. 0. 0
	3 pound of the best Sealing Wax 300 of the best Dutch Pens and 2 large Boxes of Letter Wafers	} 2. 6. 6
	A fine large Brass Frame with Candls and two Razor Mettall Penknives	} 2. 5. 0
	Two Reames of Superfine large Dutch post in 4to Cut and One Ream of fine large Dutch Post gilt in 4to	} 3. 10. 0
	More Delivered to Sir Thomas Duppa for ye use of the House of Peers	
	Two Reames of the finest horn folio Cut and folded and a Bag of Sand	} 2. 1. 0
	Two leather Bottles with Inck two Reams of the finest horn Cut and folded	} 4. 7. 0
	One ream of superfine large Dutch Post in 4to Cut and folded and one of the finest large Gilt in 4to	} 2. 10. 0

[p. 128]

		li s d
October 22th	Two Reams of Superfine horn Cutt & folded Two Reams of the finest large Dutch Post 4to Gilt Two Reames of the same Cutt and folded	} 7. 0. 0
	One Ream of the finest Horn in 4to Gilt	} 1. 0. 0
	Two Reams of the small Dutch Post 4to Cut and folded	} 1. 10. 0
	3 hundred of the best Dutch Pens a large Box of Wafers a pound of the best perfumed Sealing Wax	} 1. 11. 6
	Two reams of the finest Dutch Post large in 4to and 2 Reames of the finest horn folio Cut and folded	} 5. 0. 0

	li	s	d
3 pund of the best Sealing Wax 300 of the best Dutch Pens and 2 large Boxes of Letter Wafers	2.	6.	6
A fine large Brass Frame with Candls and two Razor Mettall Penknives	2.	5.	0
Two Reames of Superfine large Dutch Post in 4to Cut and folded and One Ream of the fine large Dutch Post	3.	10.	0

More delivered to Sir Thomas Duppa for ye use of the House of Peers

	li	s	d
Two Reames of the finest horn folio Cut and folded and a Bag of Sand	2.	1.	6
Two leather Bottles with Inck two reames of the finest horn Cut and folded	4.	7.	0
One ream of superfine large Dutch Post in 4to Cut and folded and one of the finest large Gilt in 4to	2.	19.	0

[p. 129]

	li	s	d
Two razor Mettal Penknives two pair of fine Siscers A Bag of large Pewter Standishes, a Bag of sand a Gross of Carnation Tape two large Brass frames	6.	16.	6
A leather Bottle with Inck and Two Reames superfine horn Cut & folded	2.	3.	6
Two Reames of the finest large Dutch Post in 4to Cut and folded One pair of Sizers and a Razor Mettal Penknife	2.	10.	0
	£49:	8.	6

William Churchill	The Stationers Bill November 16th 1699 for the use of the House of Lords[231]
	Delivered to Mr Aston[232]
8	Ream superfine Dutch Paper
4	Ditto Gilt
4	Ream superfine large 4to Cut and folded
4	Ditto Gilt
500	Best Dutch Pens 6 pound of Wax
3	pound Superfine Sealing Wax 8 leather Bottles Inck
4	Bags Sand 6 Boxes Wafers
12	Pen Knives 12 Pair of Sizers
20	large Pewter Standishes
4	Small Dutch Spunges and Cotton
3	Gross of Tape 6 Ivory Folders
3	Room superfine large 8vo Gilt
10	Brass Frames filled with Candls

---

[231] William Churchill's bill of 16 Nov. 1699 is duplicated, with some minor palaeographic changes, A i–ii.
[232] See Appendix: Biographical Notes.

[p. 130]

 1 Turky leather Trunck Gilt over the lock and Key double Gilt with Gold
 1 large hair Trunck
 1 Paper Book 6 Quire with Strings
10 Almancks Gilt
 2 Oxon Almanacks[233] Japan Frams
 1 Tortoise Shell Penknif with Sizers and Shag Case
   I doe hereby acknowledge to have received of Mr William Churchill the
   several things aboue mentioned for the seruice of the House of Peers
   Witness my hand this day of [blank] 1699

F Aston

[p. 131]

Die Mercurij 6° Decembris 1699[234]

Order to black rod, to bring Lieutenant Colonel John Livesey; signed by Matthew Johnson, clerk of the parliaments

Die Jovis 7 December 1699[235]

Order to black rod, for the discharge of Lieutenant Colonel John Livesey; signed by Matthew Johnson, clerk of the parliaments

[p. 132]

Die Lunae 11 Decembris 1699[236]

Order that Matthew Smith (in custody of black rod) do deliver letters and pass to the clerk of the parliaments; signed by Matthew Johnson, clerk of the parliaments

[p. 133]

19 December 1699

Received this 19th day of December 1699 of David Davis[237] the Body of Mathew Smith Esquire in to my Custody pursuant to an Order of the Right Honourable the House of Peers, Directed to the Black Rod his Deputy or Deputies by me.

William Taylor Keeper of the

Gatehouse

---

[233] The almanac published annually for the University of Oxford.

[234] *LJ*, xvi, 481.

[235] *LJ*, xvi, 482.

[236] The correct date for this order is 15 Dec. 1699. *LJ*, xvi, 485.

[237] Probably brother of Walter Davis. Born c.1662. Doorkeeper of the house of lords 1690–1710; groom of the poultry 1692–d. Died 25 Oct. 1716. *RWA*, 287 n. 5; *CTB*, ix, 780, 1732; *ORH*, ii, 96; TNA, T 53/28, p. 200.

[loose item 1][238]

57[239]

The King being not in a condition to come to this house and passe bills Mr Aston was sent twice with the following Message.[240]

Mr Speaker the King hath granted a commission under the great seale for passing the Royal Assent to those bills which have been agreed to by both Houses of parliament. And the Lords Commissioners by the King desire that this house would presently come up with their Speaker to the House of peers, to be present at the passing thereof.

[unpaginated Ai][241]

Tuesday July 7th 1702 I was sworn Gentleman Usher dayly wayter to Queen Anne[242]

Earl of Jersey July 8th my Lord Chamberleyn told me before Sir John Stanly[243] his Secretary that he had layd before the Queen my desire to be placed in the Establishment next after Sir David Mitchell for that I did fear it might be some prejudice to me. *I having been ye Eldest Gentleman Usher next ye Black Rod, and his deputy for at least 3 years.*[244] To which she was pleased to answer that tho she had put Mr Owls[245] before me as having been herr and her Sons servant yet it should be not preiudice to me in my right to the Black Rod and he ordered Sir John Stanly to make entry accordingly in his Office books At the same time he said it was the Queens order That the Gentlemen Usher shall receive noe fees for the Swearing the Servants into the house, during the first filling up the family.[246]

July 9th   I kissed ye Queens hand and wayted on the prince[247] before her going to Windsor.

---

[238] Loose leaf. It is written in the same hand as the following two entries (unpaginated Ai and loose item 2). The facts that they disclose reveal Francis Aston as the author.

[239] *Sic.*

[240] William III gave the royal assent by commission on only two occasions, 2 and 7 Mar. 1702. *LJ*, xvii, 52, 60. Following his convalescence after his horse had stumbled on 21 Feb. 1702, the king succumbed to an ailment which on 5 Mar. was diagnosed as pulmonary fever. He died on 8 Mar.

[241] Written in the same hand as loose items 1 and 2.

[242] Having been originally appointed gentleman usher daily waiter in 1692, Aston was reappointed on the accession of Anne.

[243] Secretary to the lord chamberlain 1697–1719. *ORH*, i, 171.

[244] The passage printed in italics appears in the margin, and is evidently meant to elucidate the preceding sentence which has been underlined. The king's appointment of Aston as deputy was formally communicated to the house of lords on 11 Feb. 1701 (*LJ*, xvi, 594), but he had evidently been in office since at least 16 Nov. 1699.

[245] William Oldes served as gentleman usher in the household of Queen Mary II. On her accession Queen Anne appointed him ahead of Francis Aston in the establishment list. As will be seen Aston's anxieties were fully justified. Knighted 1710. Died 5 Nov. 1718. *ORH*, i, 40 n. 4, 117; *WAR*, 188 n. 10, 230; TNA, LC 5/166, p. 80.

[246] A contemporary term frequently used to denote the royal household.

[247] George of Denmark.

The same day my warrant for the Gentleman Usher bears date.[248]

[loose item 2][249]

That it is the Queens order that the Gentleman usher shall recieve noe fees for His Swearing the Servants in the lords during the first filling up the Family.

[loose item 2 dorse]

Anno 1713

My finding this entry on the other side gives me an occasion of mentioning what followed 9 years after.[250]

When Sir David Michel was dead[251] I went to the Queen and asked his place, the Queen sayd she would send me an answer by my Lord Chamberleyn I wayted on my Lord Shrewsbury next morning when [he] told me ye Queen had given the Black Rod to Mr Owls who she sayd was my senior (or to that effect) upon which I told the Duke of Shrewsbury my story that I had been Gentleman Usher since the the Revolution and dayly wayter Since 1691,[252] and Mr Owls was made since the Queen came to the Crown.

That upon the Queen making the Establishment of the family she had put Mr Owls his name before mine, upon which I drew up a petition to her majesty desiring that my name might be writt in the Establishment next Sir David Michel, least it might be found prejudicial to me in my pretensing to the black Rod. this petition I shewd (Lawrence) the Earl of Rochester, who took it and gave it to my Lord Jersy to lay before the Queen, which was done, and the answer given on ye other side. when my Lord Shrewsbury heard this he said it was quite contrary to what the Queen saide I answerd that what I sayd was litteraly said my Lord Rochester & my Lord Jersey were then both alive.

[Reverse end and turned upside down]

[unpaginated Aii][253]

Mr Churchills Bill November 16th 1699 for the Use of the House of Lords Delivered to Mr Aston[254]

8	Ream Superfine Dutch Paper
4	Ditto Gilt
4	Ream superfine large 4to Cut & Folded
4	Ditto Gilt
500	Best Dutch Pens[255]
3	lb Superfine Sealing Wax 8 – Leather Bottles Inck
4	Bags Sand – 6 Boxes Wafers

---

[248] *Sic.*

[249] In the same hand as loose item 1 and unpaginated Ai.

[250] Evidently written by Aston on finding his earlier note.

[251] Mitchel died on 1 June 1710. *ODNB.*

[252] Aston was appointed gentleman usher daily waiter in Mar. 1691/2. *ORH*, i, 68.

[253] Written in a different hand.

[254] This is a duplicate of William Churchill's bill of 16 Nov. 1699 (pp. 71–2) with minor variants.

[255] '6 pound of Wax' (p. 71) omitted.

12	Penknives – 12 Pair of Sizers
20	Large Pewter Standishes
4	Small Dutch Spunges & Cotton
3	Gross of Tape – 6 Ivory Folders
3	Ream superfine large 8vo Gilt
10	Brass Frames filled with Candls
1	Turky leather Trunck Gilt over The lock & Key double Gilt with Gold
1	Large hair Trunck
1	Paper Book 6 Quire with Strings
10	Almanacks gilt
2	Oxon Almanacks Japan Frams
1	Tortoise shell Penknive with Sizers & Shaggreen Case

I doe hereby acknowledge, I have received of Mr William Churchill the several things

[unpaginated Aiii]

aboue mentioned for the Seruice of the House of Peers Witnesse my hand this day of [blank]

To Mr Snow[256] for the Lord Chancellors Lord Treasurers and the Bishops Roomes

S	3}		Andirons 4
P	1}	Frames 2	Papers – Inck – Sand – Wax
W	1}	Sand 1	Wafers – Inckes – Penknife
I	1}	P	Sizers – and an Almanack

To Mr Hancock for the Earl Marshalls Room

Standish – 1 And other things

To Mr Windham for the Robe Room and for Conferences in the Painted Chamber

3 Standishes &c

To Mr Smart[257]   1 Standish &c

To Mr Burk[258]   1 Standish &c

To Mr Walter Davis[259] for my Lord Privy Seal's Room

1 Standish &c

[unpaginated Aiv]

---

[256] Either John or William Snow, doorkeepers of the house of lords 1665–81. *CTB*, i, 646; vii, 177; viii, 491.

[257] John Smart, doorkeeper of the house of lords 1677–92. *CTB*, v, 726; ix, 1732.

[258] Probably David Bourke, doorkeeper of the house of lords 1695. *CTB*, x, 1200.

[259] Probably brother of David Davis. Doorkeeper of the house of lords 1690–1720. *RWA*, 287 n. 5; *CTB*, ix, 1732; TNA, T53/28, p. 200.

To David Davis for my Lord Great Chamberlain's[260]
most Committees Sitt and that Lobby

The Prince's Room where
6 Standishes and other things
proportionable

The Yeoman Usher a Standish Paper &c

An Inventory of the Furniture left in the House of Peers at the Rising of
the House on Tuesday the 11th of April 1700[261]

10	Turky Work Chairs	} In the Lord Great Chamberlain's Room
1	Table and Carpet	
1	Close stool & Pan	} In the Princes Room
20	Turky Work Chairs	
1	Table and Carpett	} In the King's Stole Room
1	Table and Carpett	
	Kings Stole	} In the Lord Chancellors Room
6	Turky Work Chairs	
1	Table and Carpett	
1	Close Stole & Pan	} In the Lord Treasurers Room
6	Turky Work Chairs	
12	Turky Work Chairs	
1	Table	} In the Bishopps Room
1	Close Stool and Pan	

[unpaginated Av]

6	Turky Work Chairs	} In the Earl Marshalls Room
1	Table and Carpett	
1	Close Stool and Pan	} In the Privy Seals Room
3	Chairs	
1	Table	
1	Close Stool and Pan	} In the Robe Room
12	Old Turky Ware Chairs	
1	Table and Carpett	
2	Close stools & Pans	} In the Black Rod
9	Turky Work Chairs	
1	Table	
1	Chair	} In the Closett
1	Table	
1	Chamber Pott	} In the Cubbord
2	Dozen and 4 large Pewter Candlestickes	
6	Snuffers & Panns	
3	Frames Wax Tapers	
6	New Chamberpotts	} In the Inner Room
4	Old Chamberpotts	
4	Old Close Stools & Panns	

[260] 'Room' omitted.

[261] In a different hand from the previous section/the bulk of the volume.

[unpaginated Avi][262]

Bill for Candles

Deliver to the Black Rod for the service of the House of Peers the usual winter allowance of Candles &c for this Month of January 1703[263]

To the Chandry	6	Dozen of white wax lights	
	12	Dozen pound of Tallow lights	per mensem
	4	Bunches of Sizes	
	2	Dozen Torches	

Bill for Wood

Deliver for the Service of the House of Peers the usual winter allowance of wood and coal for the Month of January 1703. viz.

Tall wood	1 load and a half	
Billetts	1000	per diem
Scotch coal	100	

Deliver for the Service of the house of Peers, the usual winter allowance of Charcoal for the Month of January 1703. viz.

Scote charcoal 1 Quarter. 4 Bushells per diem

Note that the Summer allowance is but half of the Winter. That the several Bills above mentiond must be underwrit by the officer of the board of Greencloth

Parliament Fees.

An Earls fee of Entrance

	li	s.	d.
Clerk of the Parliament	4	0	0
Gentleman Usher Black Rod	4	0	0
Clerk assistent	2	10	0
Yeoman Usher	2	10	0
8 Door Keepers	2	0	0
	15:	0	0

A Barons fee of Entrance

		li	s.	d.
Clerk of the Parliament		2:	10:	0
Gentleman Usher Black rod		2:	10:	0
Clerk assistent		0:	10:	0
Yeoman Usher		0:	10:	0
8 Door Keepers		2:	0:	0
		8:	0:	0

Private Bill fee

	li	s.	d.
Speaker	10	0	0
Black rod	5	0	0
Clericus Parliamenti	5	0	0
Clerk Assistent	2	10	0
Yeoman Usher	2	10	0

	li	s.	d.
8 door Keepers	2	0	0
an Order	0	10	0
	27	10	0

XN a double Bill pays as much more than a single

Item a Bill of Naturalization the Clerk of the Crown has 1li 5s for swearing each person

---

[262] Written in a different hand.

[263] 1703/4.

[unpaginated Avii]

Ingrossing of Bills

For the first presse[264]	0	13	4
for each of the <u>rest</u>	0	10	0

	Causes at the Bar		
Black Rod	2	0	0
Clerk Assistent	1	0	0
Yeoman Usher	1	0	0
8 Door Keepers	3	0	0
	7	0	0
Prisoners fee			
Clerk of Parliament	3	6	8
Black Rod	3	6	8
Clerk assistent	1	0	0
Yeoman usher	1	0	0
Order of discharge	0	14	6
Reading a petition	0	2	0
	9	9	10

To the Black Rod for Custody 20s. or 13s. 4d. per diem

---

[264] Reading uncertain.

Appendix: Biographical Notes

Arlington, Henry Bennett (1618–85), earl of
MP 1661–5; secretary of state 1662–74; PC 1662-*d*. *cr*. Baron Arlington 1665, earl of Arlington 1672. Lord chamberlain of the household 1674-*d*. KG 1672.

Aston, Francis (1644/5–1715)
b. 1644/45, yr s. of Francis Aston of the parish of St Mary-le-Strand, Mdx. *educ*. Westminster Sch. adm. by 1656, king's scholar 1660; Trinity Coll., Camb. adm. 1661, BA 1665, fellow 1667, MA 1668. Travelled on the continent 1669. *unm*. FRS 1678. Councillor of Royal Society 1680–1, frequently 1699–*d*., secretary 30 Nov. 1681, resigned 9 Dec. 1685; gentleman usher quarterly waiter 1689, daily waiter 1692; deputy black rod by 1696. On the accession of Anne in 1702 she appointed William Oldes daily waiter over Aston: this cost him the seniority which eight years later might have led to his appointment as black rod. *d*. mid July 1715. H.G. Lyons, 'Biographical Notes', *Notes and Records of the Royal Society*, iii (1940), 88–92; *ORH*, i, 68; *LJ*, xvi, 59; TNA, PROB 11/547, sig. 127.

Ayton, Sir John (*d*. 1681)
Nephew of Sir Robert Ayton (1570–1638), secretary to Queens Anne of Denmark and Henrietta Maria. Gentleman usher to Charles, prince of Wales; gentleman usher daily waiter 1660–72; black rod 1671–5. Knighted by 1661. *ORH*, i, 68; *RWA*, 191 n 1.

Browne, John (*d*. 1691)
s. of Thomas Browne, grocer of London. *educ*. M. Temple. *m*. (1) Temperance, da. of Sir Thomas Crewe of Steane, Northants; (2) Elizabeth, da. of John Packer of Shillingford, Berks. Clerk of the parliaments 1638–49, 1660-*d*. Buried at Eydon, Northants, 8 June 1691. *ODNB*.

Carteret, Sir Edward (*d*. 1683)
Gentleman usher daily waiter 1660; deputy black rod 1661; black rod 1671. Knighted by 1661. *d*. 1683. *ORH*, i, 83; *RWA*, 192 n. 1.

Duppa, Sir Thomas (1619–94)
b. 2 Apr. 1619, o.s. of John Duppa of Eardisley, Herefs. *educ*. DCL, Oxf. 1670. *m*. Joan, da. of William Wheeler, goldsmith, of St Martin-in-the-Field, Mdx. Servant of Charles, prince of Wales; gentleman usher quarterly waiter 1660, daily waiter assistant 1662, daily waiter 1671; deputy black rod 1675; black rod 1683-*d*. Knighted 6 May 1683. *d*. 25 Apr. 1694. Buried in Westminster Abbey. *RWA*, 234 n. 3; *ORH*, i, 99–100; TNA, PROB 11/419, sig. 75.

Harsnett, Sir Roger (*d.* 1692)
m. Carola, da. of Robert Barne of Great Grimsby, Lincs. Serjeant at arms 1660–*d.*, assigned to speaker of the house of lords 1689. Major, Sir William Killigrew's regiment of foot 1662. Knighted by 1689. Deputed by black rod to execute warrants 1690. *d.* 25 Oct. 1692. Buried in Westminster Abbey. *ORH*, i, 40 n 4, 117; *CTB*, x, 306; *RWA*, 188 n 10, 230 n 8; *English Army Lists*, ed. C. Dalton (6 vols, 1904), i, 24.

Johnson, Matthew (1637–1723)
Baptised 8 Sept. 1637, e.s. of Templer Johnson of Gretton, Northants. *educ.* M. Temple; adm. 1662. Called 1671, bencher 1691. *m.* Margaret, da. of Edward Palmer. Clerk of the patents to Attorney General Palmer by 1668–70; clerk of the parliaments 1691–1716. *d.* 13 Dec. 1723. J.C. Sainty, *The Parliament Office in the Seventeenth and Eighteenth Centuries: Biographical Notes on Clerks in the House of Lords 1600 to 1800* (House of Lords Record Office, 1977), 17.

Lindsey, Robert Bertie (1630–1701), 3rd earl of
MP 1661–6. *succ.* as 3rd earl 1666. Lord great chamberlain 1666–*d.*; PC 1666–79, resworn 1682–*d.*

Maxwell, James (*d.* 1650)
Gentleman usher daily waiter 1603; groom of the bedchamber 1620; black rod 1620–49. *cr.* earl of Dirletoun [S] 1646. *d.* 19 Apr. 1650. J.C. Sainty, 'A Biographical Note on James Maxwell, Gentleman Usher of the Black Rod', *Parliamentary History* (forthcoming).

Montagu, Ralph (1638–1708), earl of
MP 1678–81. *succ.* as 3rd Baron Montagu of Boughton 1684. Master of the horse to Queen Catherine of Braganza 1665–78; master of the great wardrobe 1671–85, 1689–*d.*; PC 1672–9, resworn 1689–*d. cr.* earl of Montagu 1689, duke of Montagu 1705.

Mulgrave, John Sheffield (1647–1721), 3rd earl of
succ. as 3rd earl of Mulgrave 1658. Lord chamberlain of the household 1685–8. *cr.* marquess of Normanby 1694, duke of Buckingham and Normanby 1703. KG 1674.

Rochester, Laurence Hyde (1642–1711), 1st earl of
2nd s. of 1st earl of Clarendon. MP 1660–80. *cr.* Viscount Hyde of Kenilworth 1681, earl of Rochester 1682. Lord of the treasury 1679, first lord 1679–84; PC 1679–88, 1692–*d.*; lord president 1684–5, 1710–*d.*; lord treasurer 1685–7; lord lieutenant [I] 1700–3. KG 1685.

Index

Numbers and references in **bold** refer to those in the original manuscript given in square brackets.